Modern Art designs of
Solid M.S. Iron bar welded with
Round and Half Round curves.

Australian design of Gate,

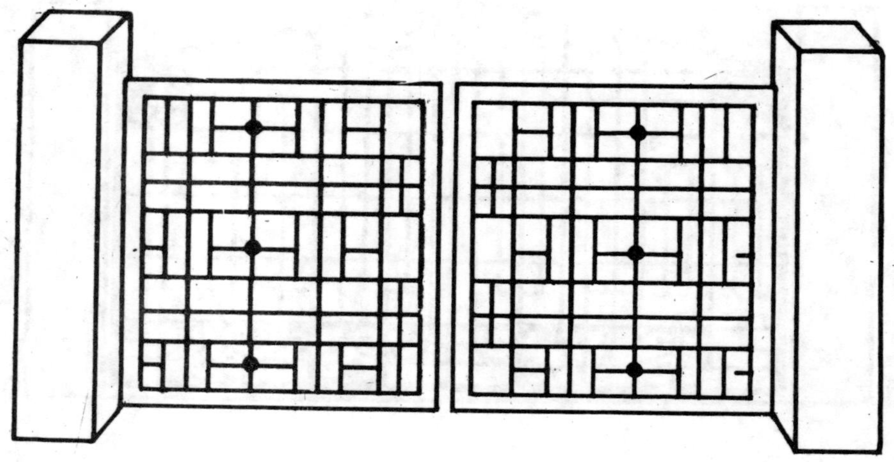

Quite Modern Big Gate design of solid Iron bars

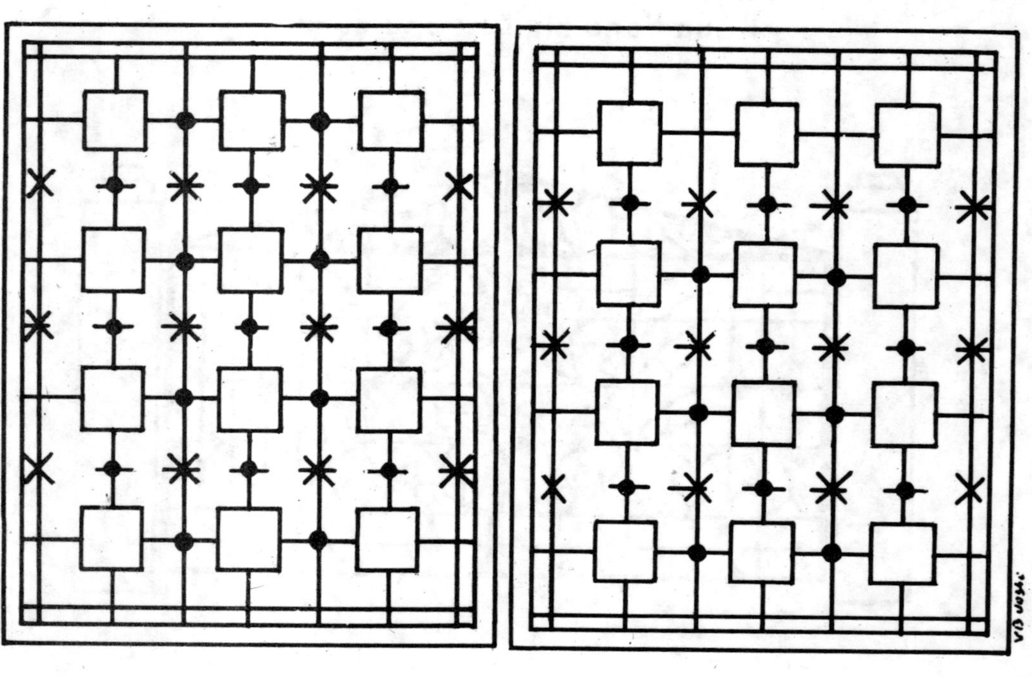

MORE AND MORE DESIGNS OF

GATES GRILLS RAILINGS & STAIRCASES

by

V. K. JOSHI

PUSTAK MAHAL®

Administrative office and sale centre
J-3/16, Daryaganj, New Delhi-110002
☎ 011-23276539, 23272783, 23272784, 23260518
E-mail: info@pustakmahal.com • *Website:* www.pustakmahal.com

Branches
Bengaluru: ☎ 080-22234025, 40912845
E-mail: pustakmahalblr@gmail.com

Mumbai: ☎ 022-22010941, 22053387
E-mail: unicornbooksmumbai@gmail.com

ISBN 978-81-223-0528-9

Edition: 2022

Printed at: Glorious Printers, Delhi

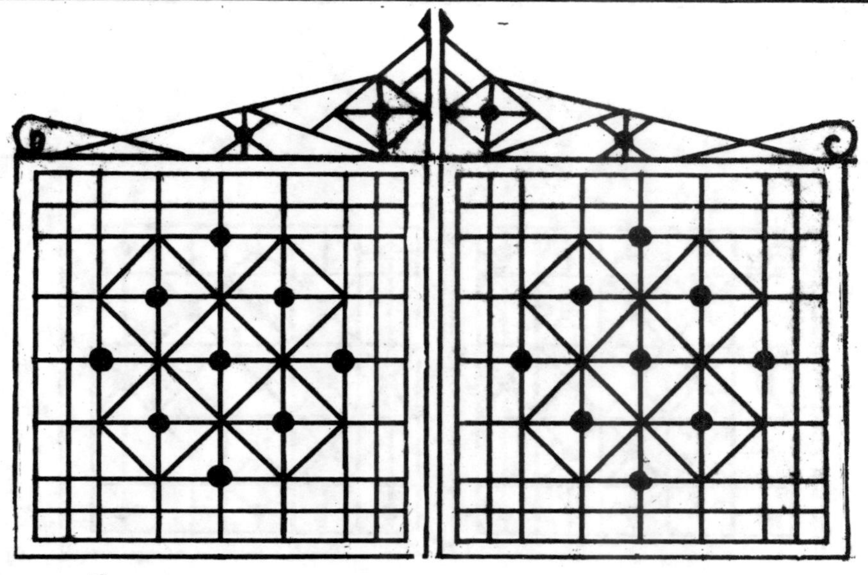

A Common design of Gates for Small and Big Factories,

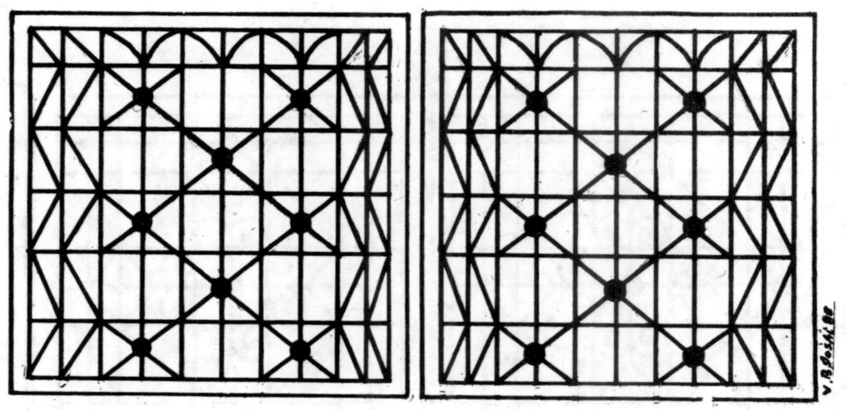

Artistic Design of Cast Iron Rod and curves

Gate

New Sample of Universal Design—Common for all types of Construction

Modern Designs of M. S. Wrought Iron Grill.

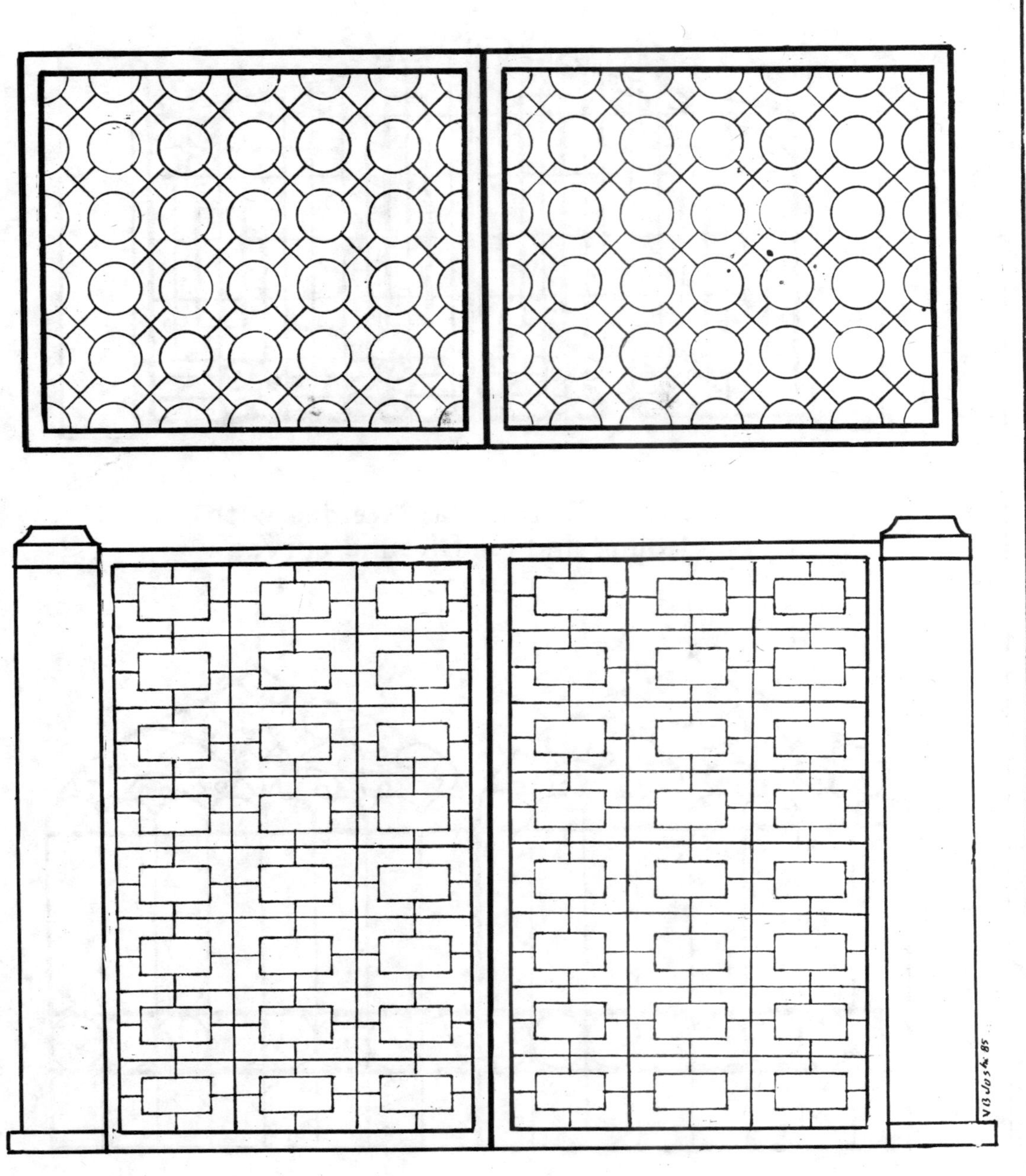

New Australian design of Gate.

Solid M.S. Iron bar welded with Round and Half Round curved designs.

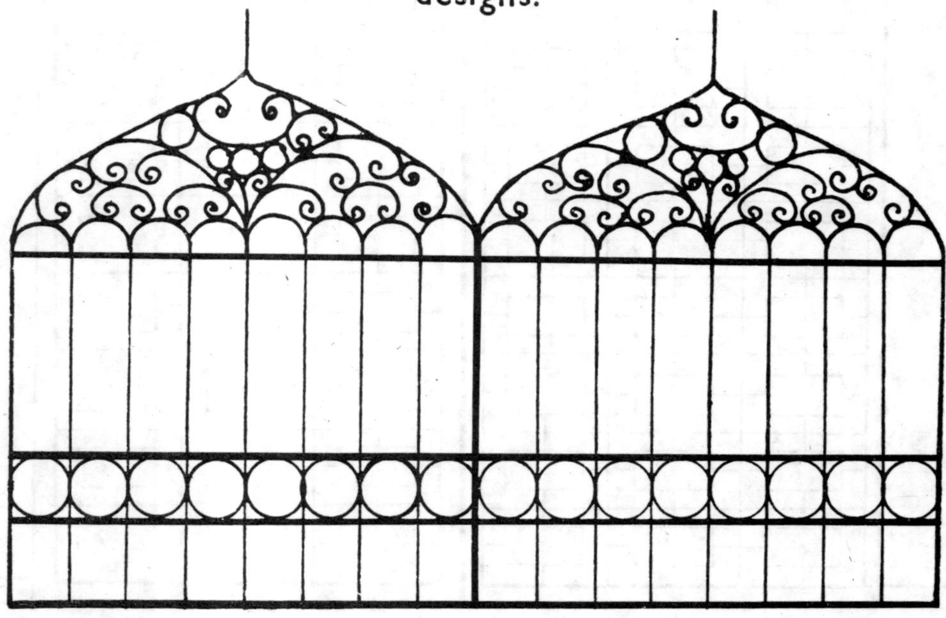

Very Cheerful design for House and

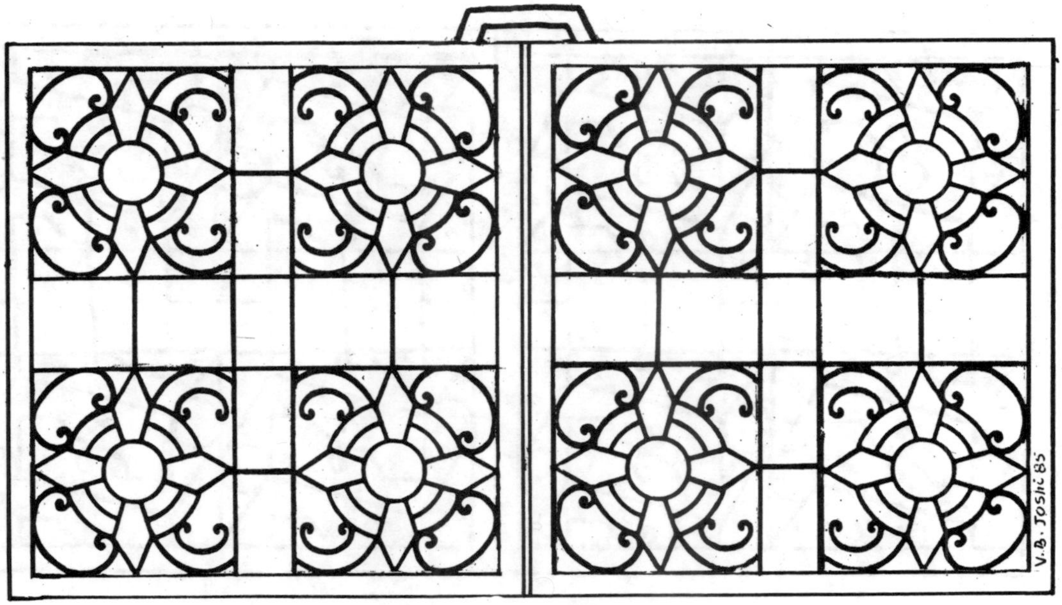

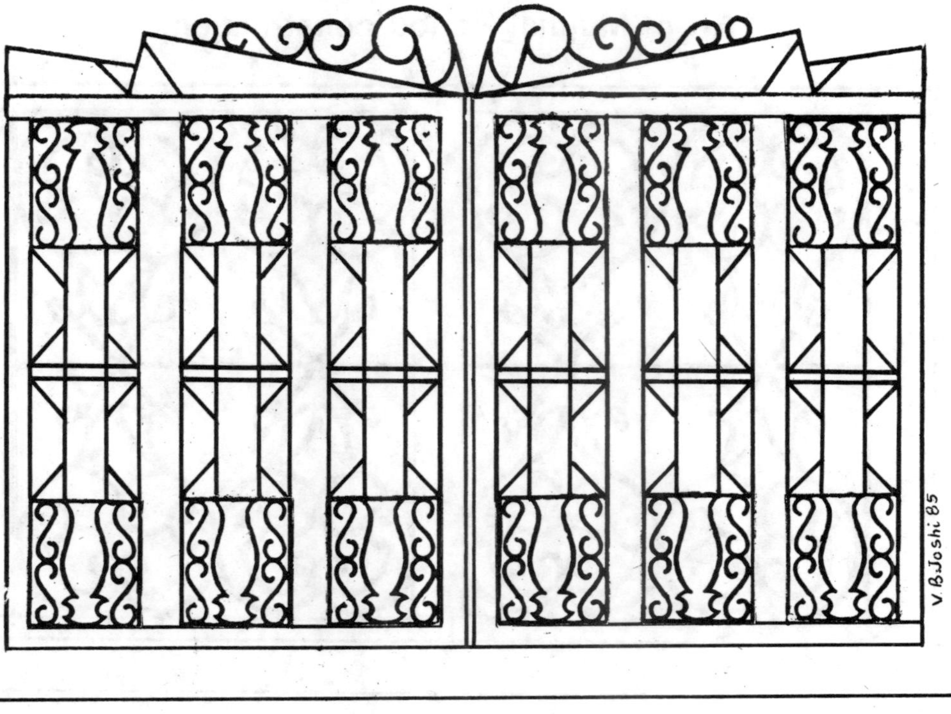

Beautiful Gates

Art of Mughal Period construction.

Japan's design for beautiful decoration.

British architectural Gate Designs of Long Iron bars

British Ancient Art designs

Germany's design of Gates for Small and Big Factories

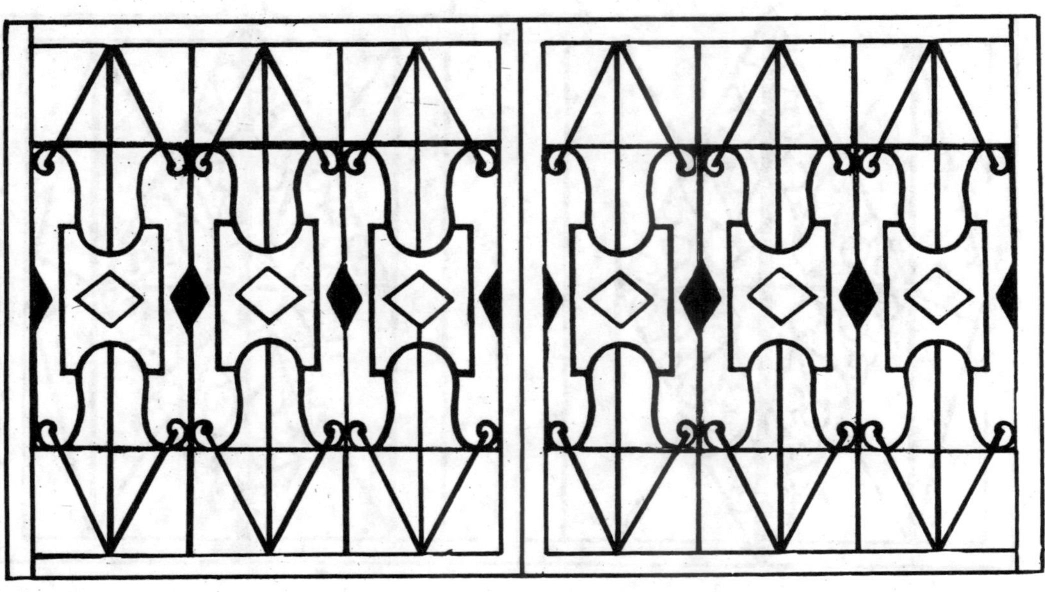

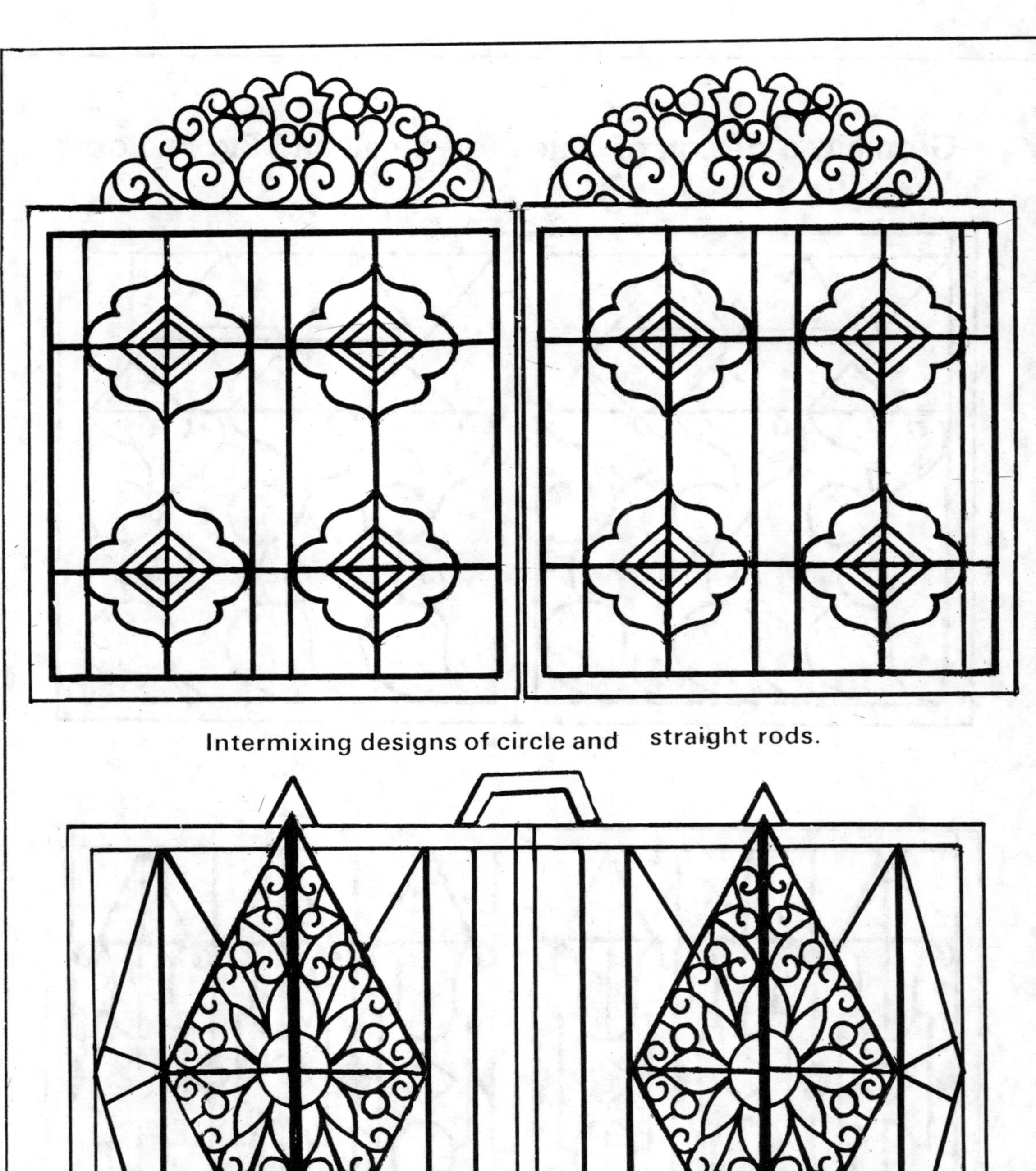

Intermixing designs of circle and straight rods.

Artistic Design of Cast Iron Rod and curves

Flower design of solid Iron bars welded in Square bar frame.

Art of Mughal Period construction.

Straight Iron bar Design.

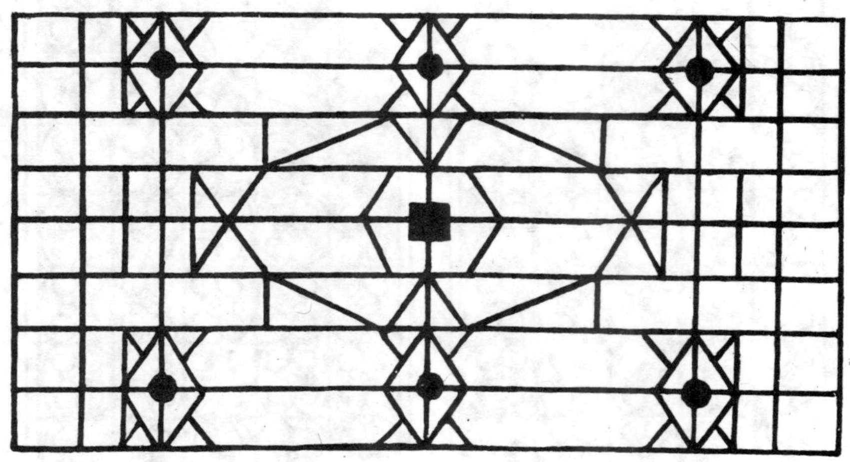

Round Iron bar designs in layer welded in Geometrical principle.

Rounded edges Designs, made of solid iron bars and hollow pipes for Decoration.

Art of Mughal Period Designs for Modern style

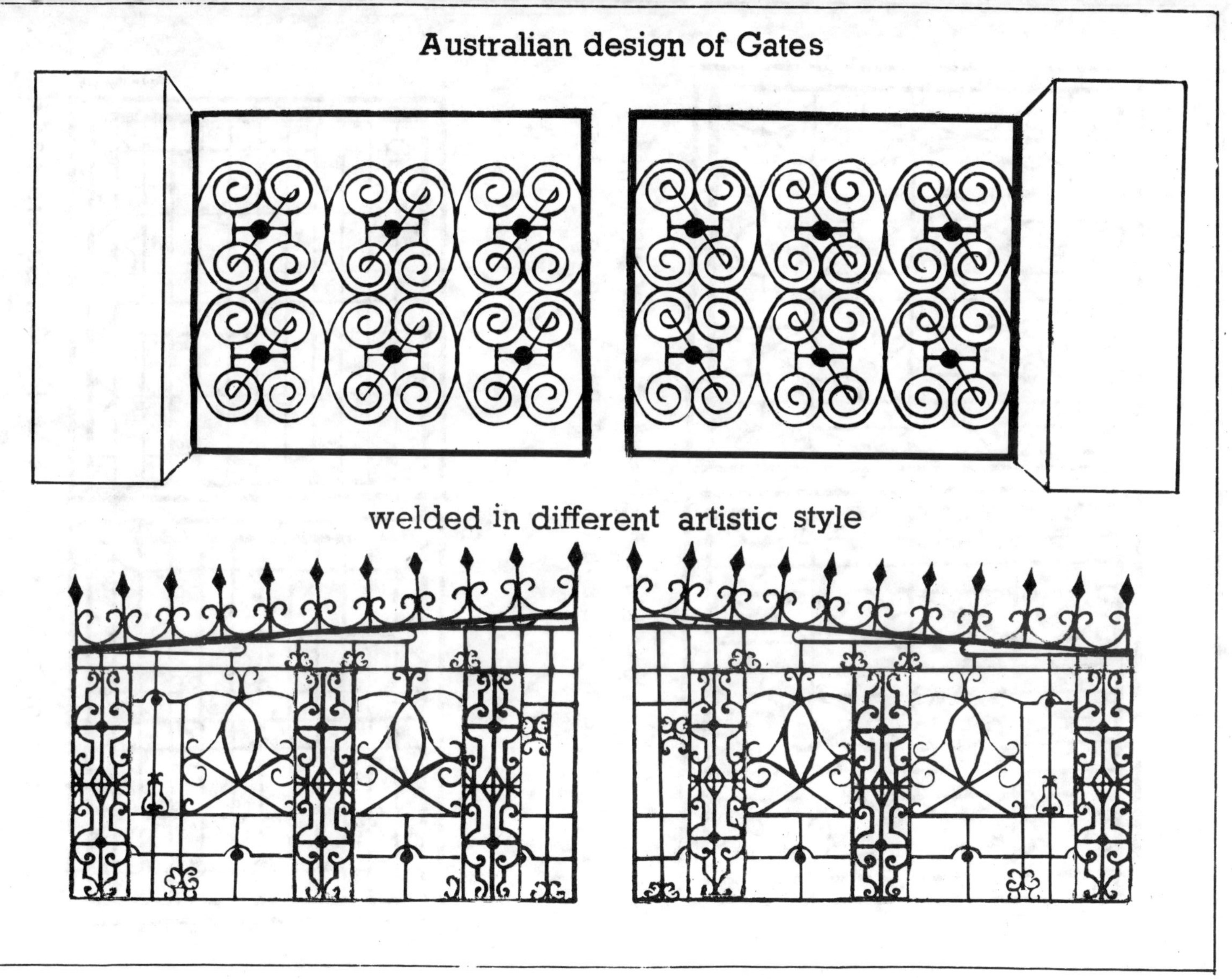

Australian design of Gates

welded in different artistic style

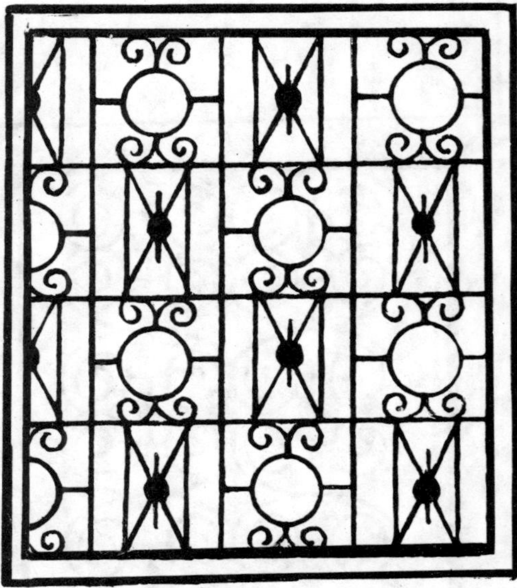

A composition of latest design with different style of Rectangular Iron bar or pipe

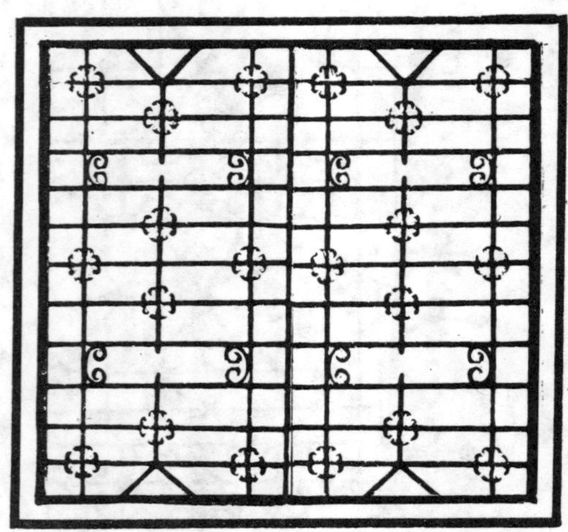

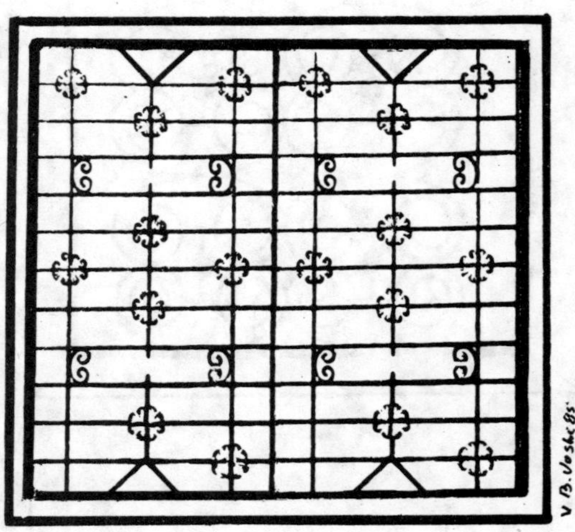

Flower design of solid Iron bars welded in Square bar frame.

Japan's design for decoration.

Ultra-modern Vertical Iron bars designs

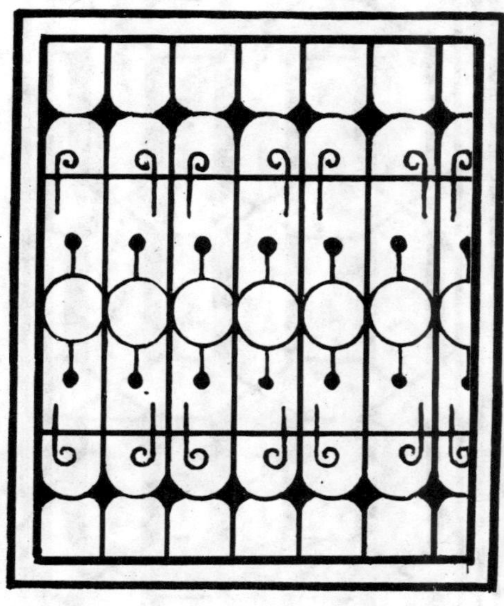

Beautiful Gate

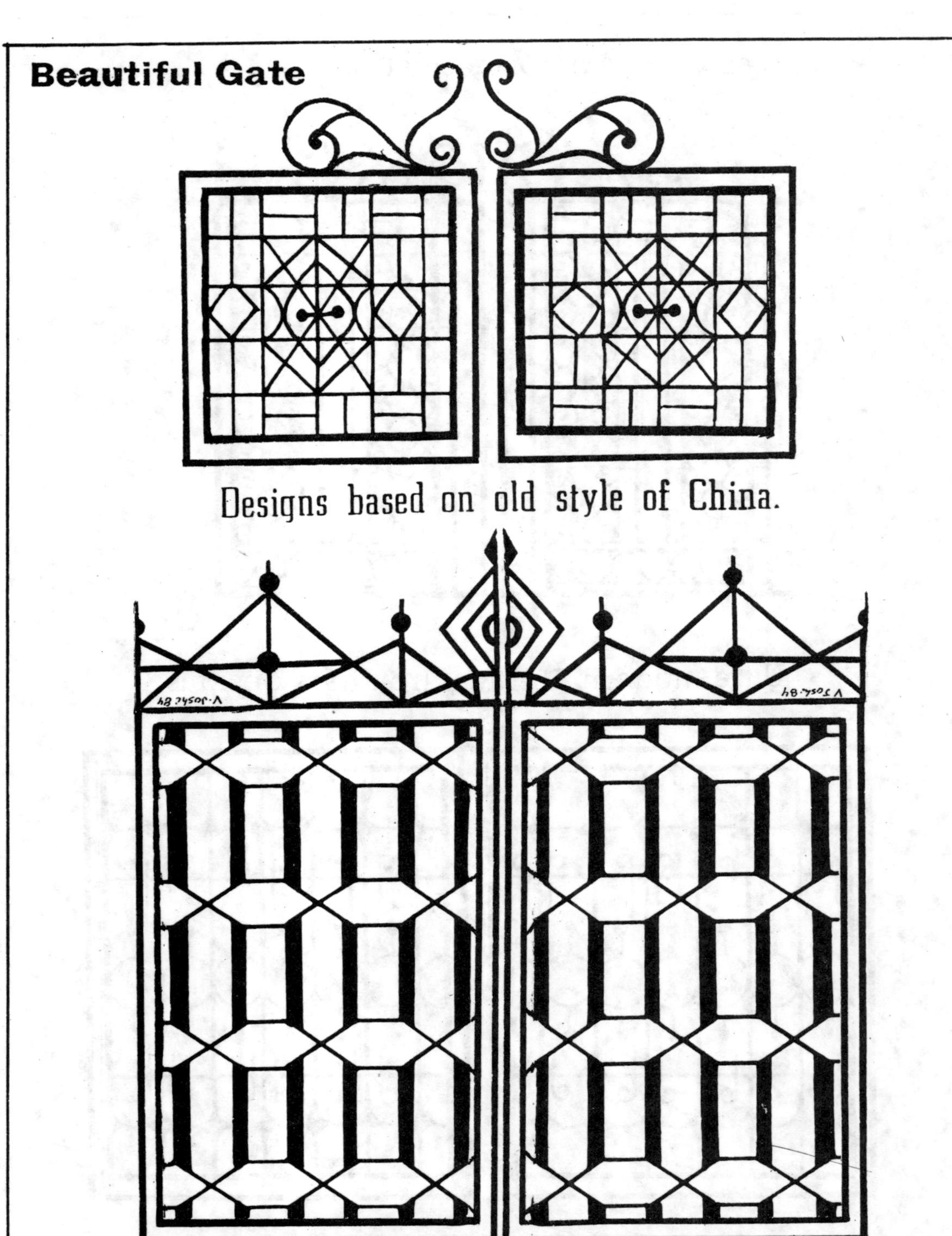

Designs based on old style of China.

Two pairs of modern designs

These designs shows the Idea of British Ancient Art suitable for office, College and School Buildings.

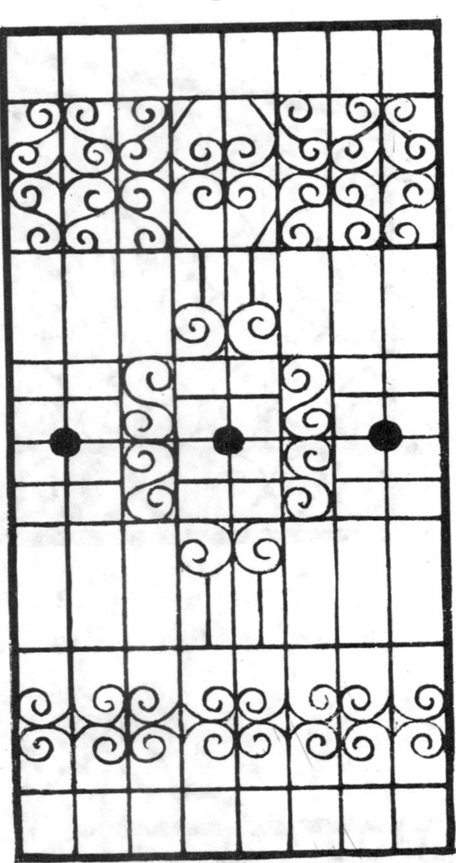

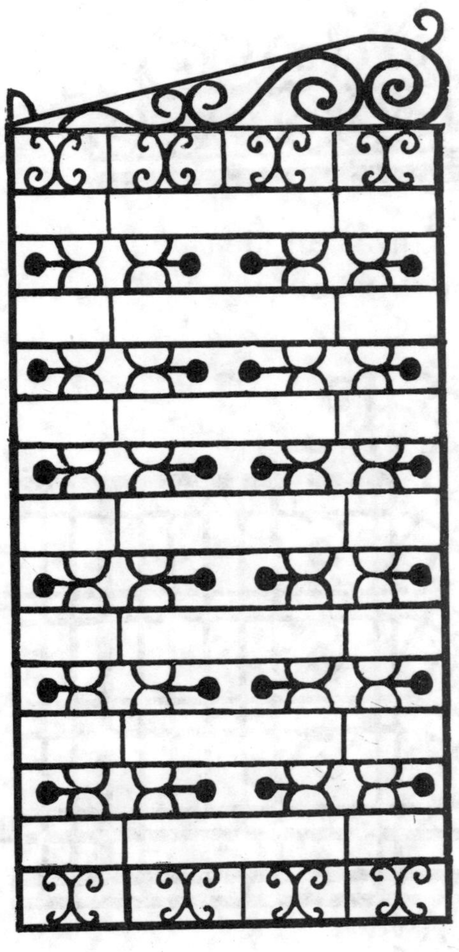

A Common design of Gates for Small and Big Factories,

Complete Ancient Design gives an idea and Art of Mughal Period construction.

Strong design of Indian style useful for Factories and Garden

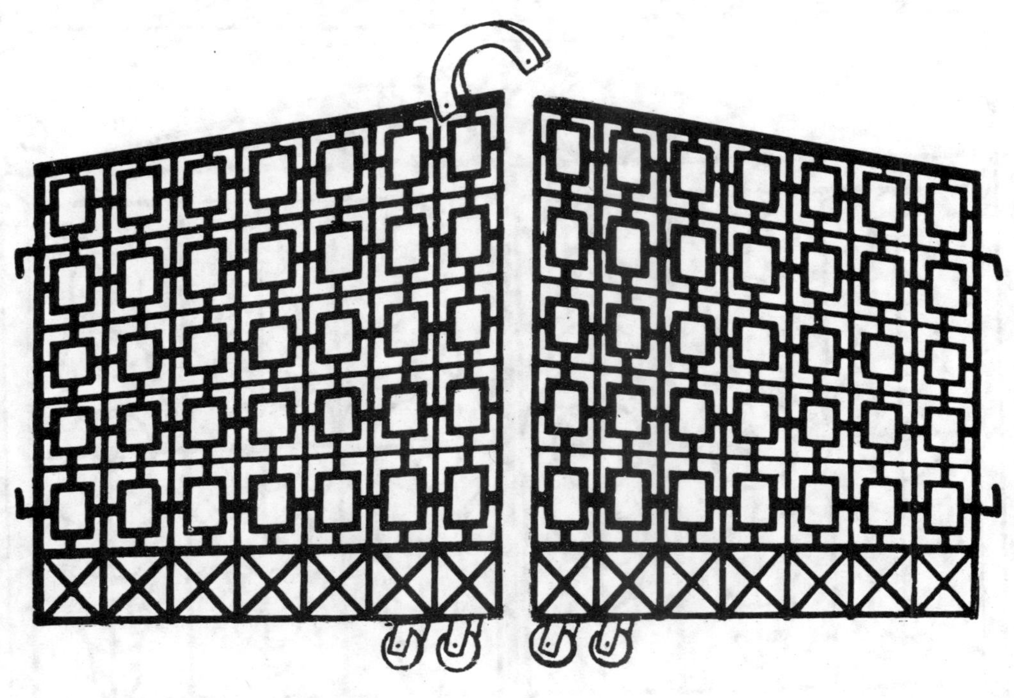

Very strong designs for decoration of residential and commercial building.

Architectural design of solid Square bar frame

Latest design Made of thick and thin solid bars welded in Geometrical style.

Gates

West Germany's Designs

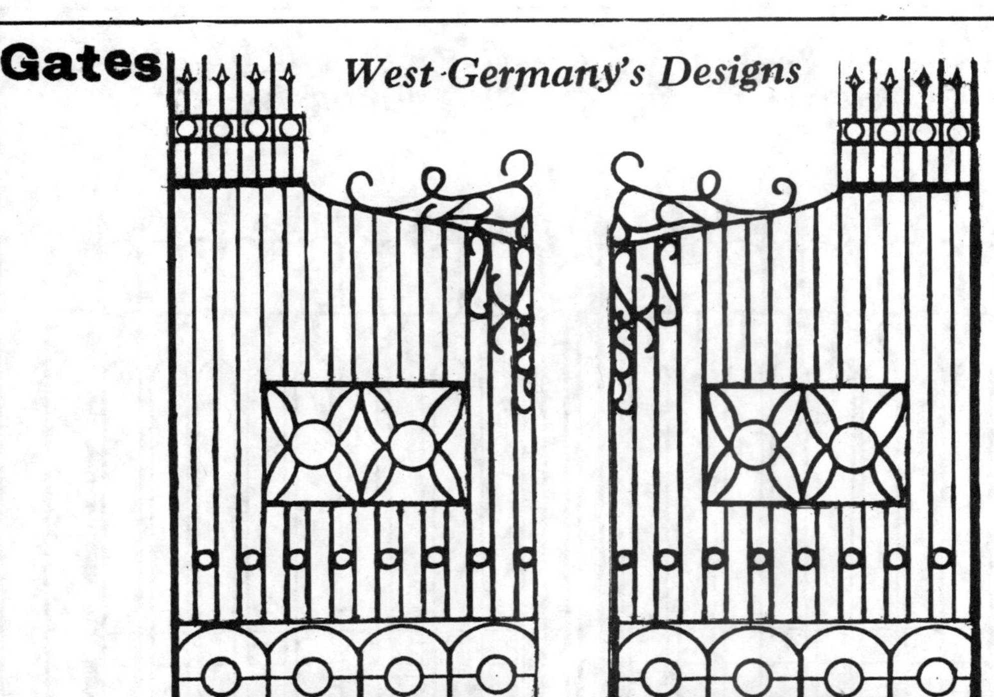

New designs welded in different artistic style

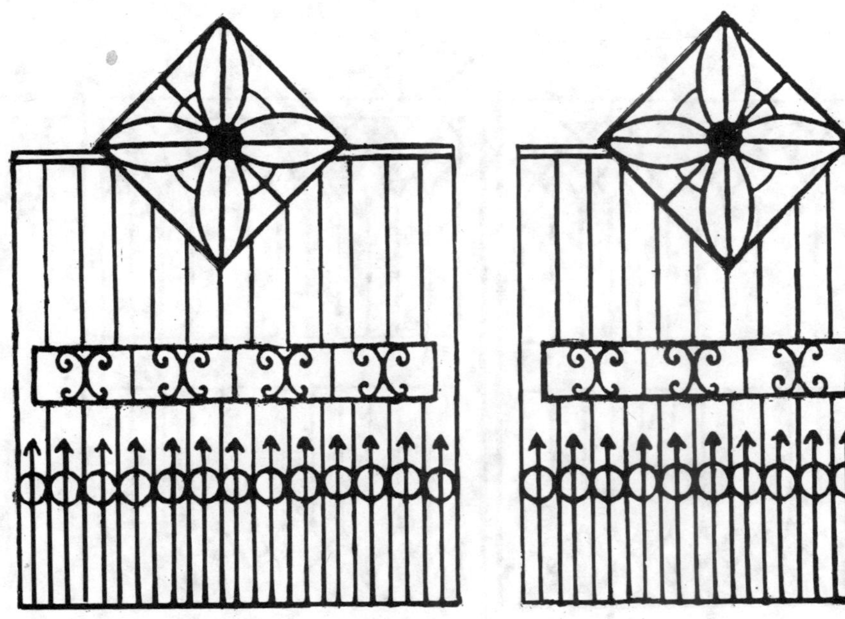

British architectural Gate Designs of Long Iron bars welded with pipes, for Big Embassy.

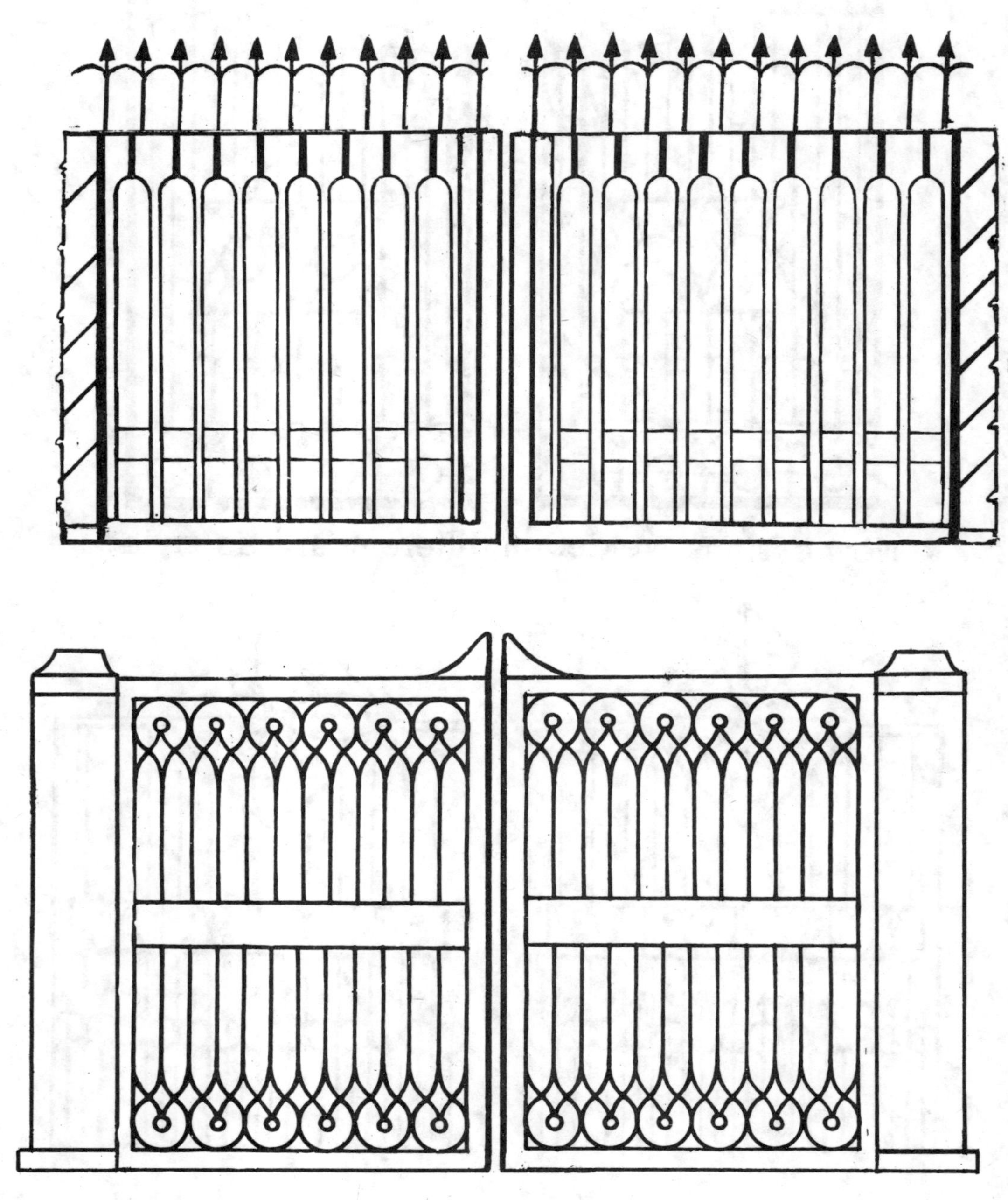

Artistic Design ot Cast Iron Rod and curve

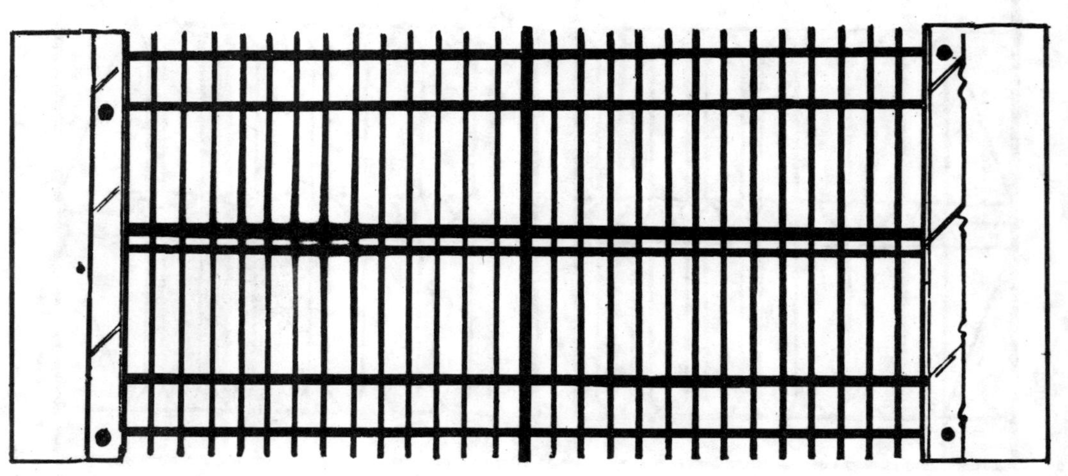

Design of Vertical Iron Bars welded with Horizontal pipe for light Construction of Railways.

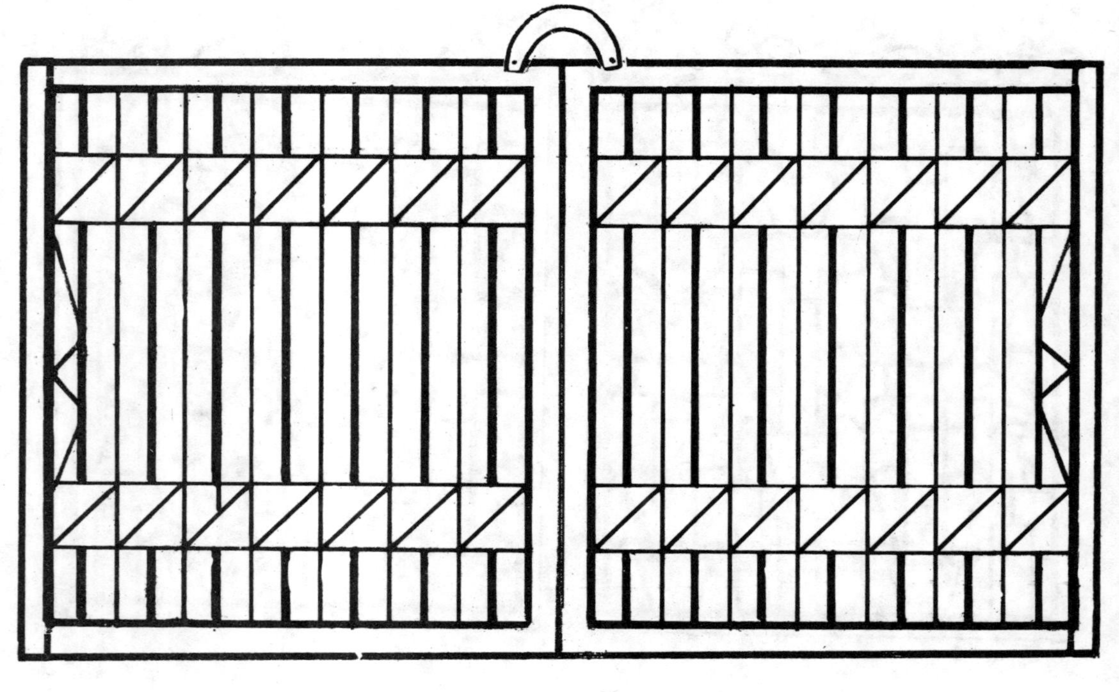

Art of Mughal Period Designs

Old Design for Strong Construction.

Australian design of Gate,
rods welded in Geometrical principle.

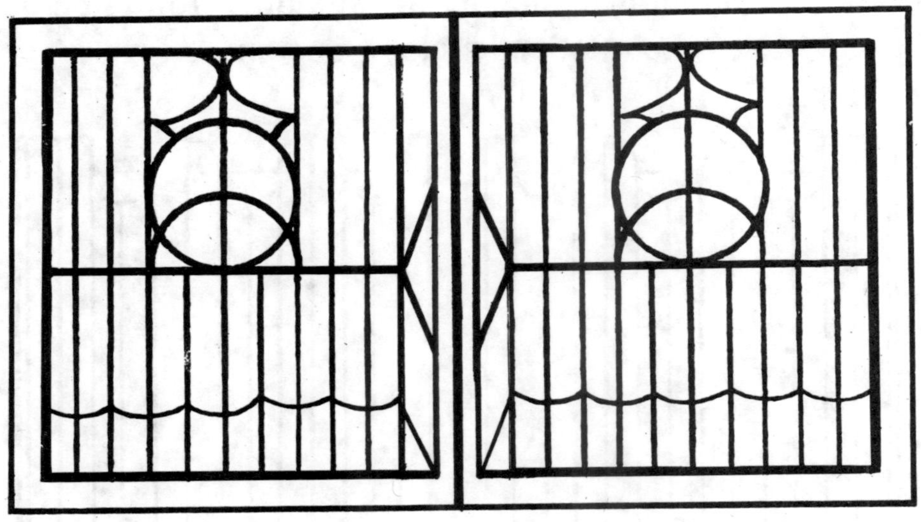

Round Iron bar designs in layer style, welded on steel frames

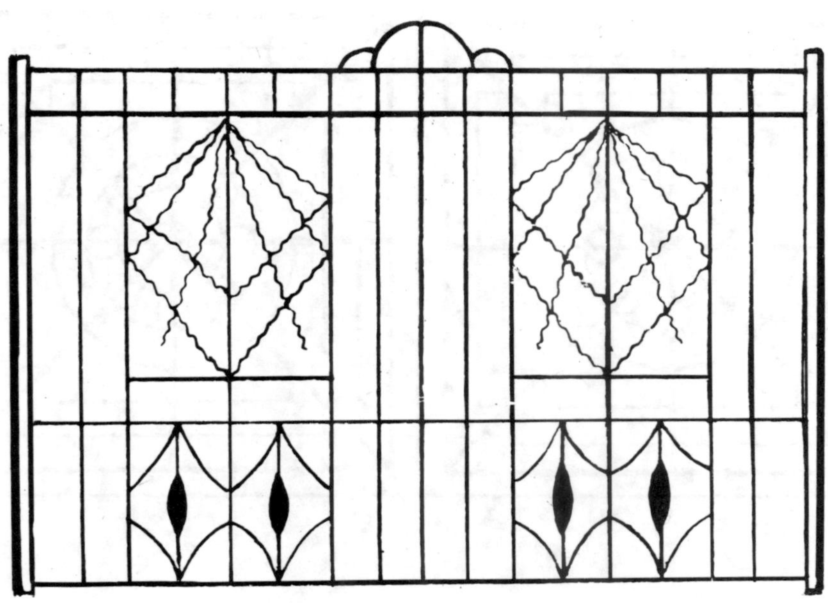

Gate

Symmitrical setting of straight Iron bars and Semicircle design.

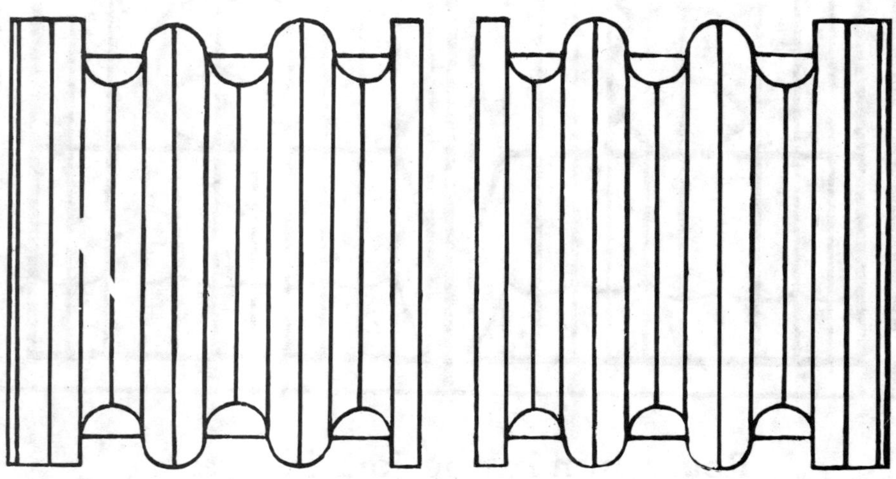

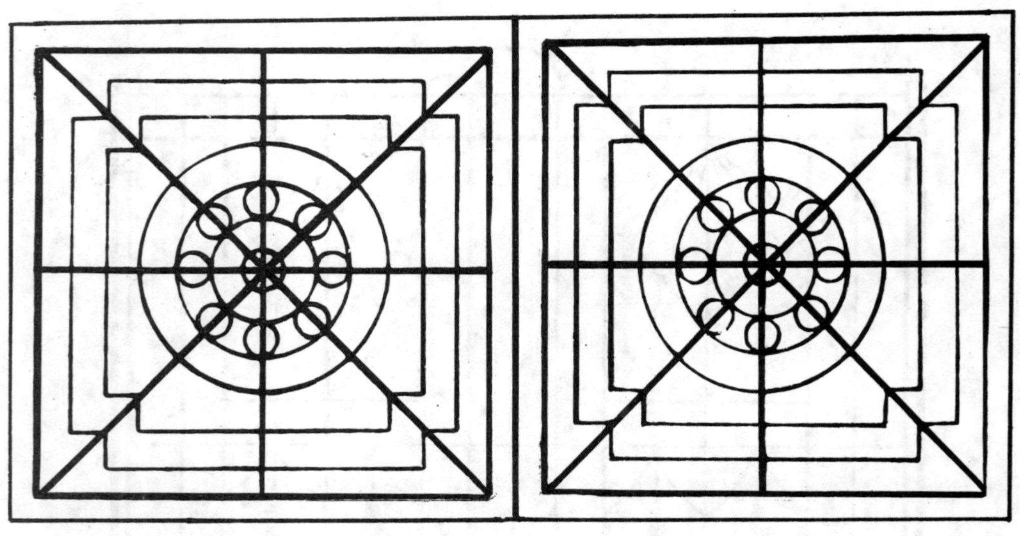

Two all purpose designs of old style.

Very simple and beautiful design of Tokyo.

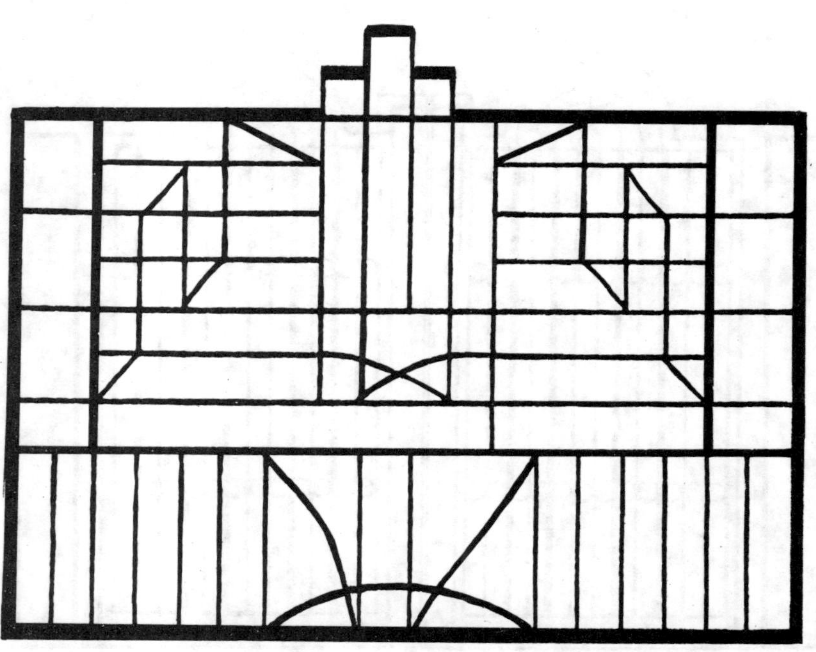

Vertical Iron bars designs for well Planned Building.

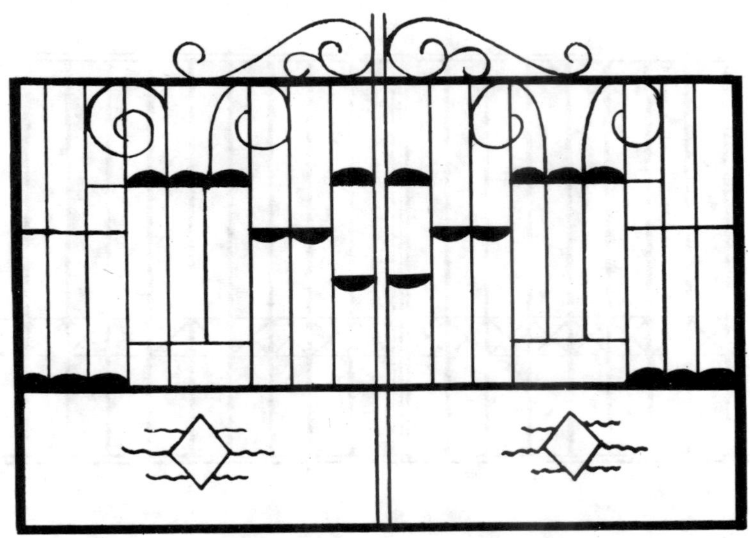

Ultra-modern Vertical Iron bars designs for well Planned Building.

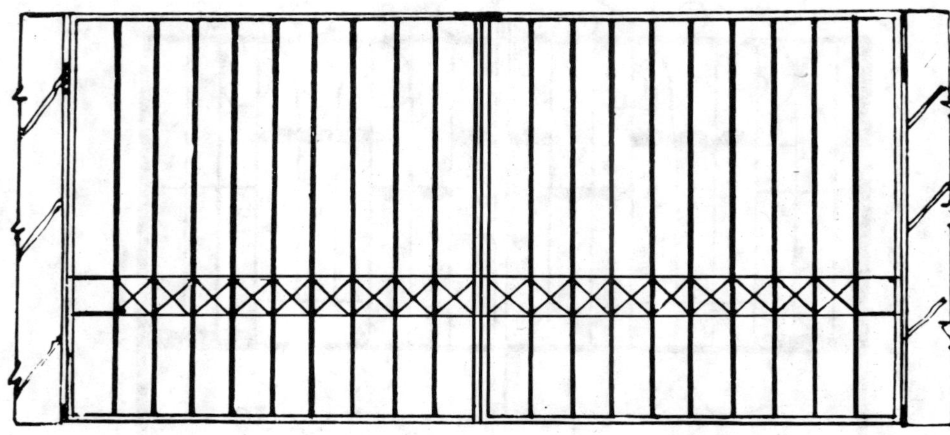

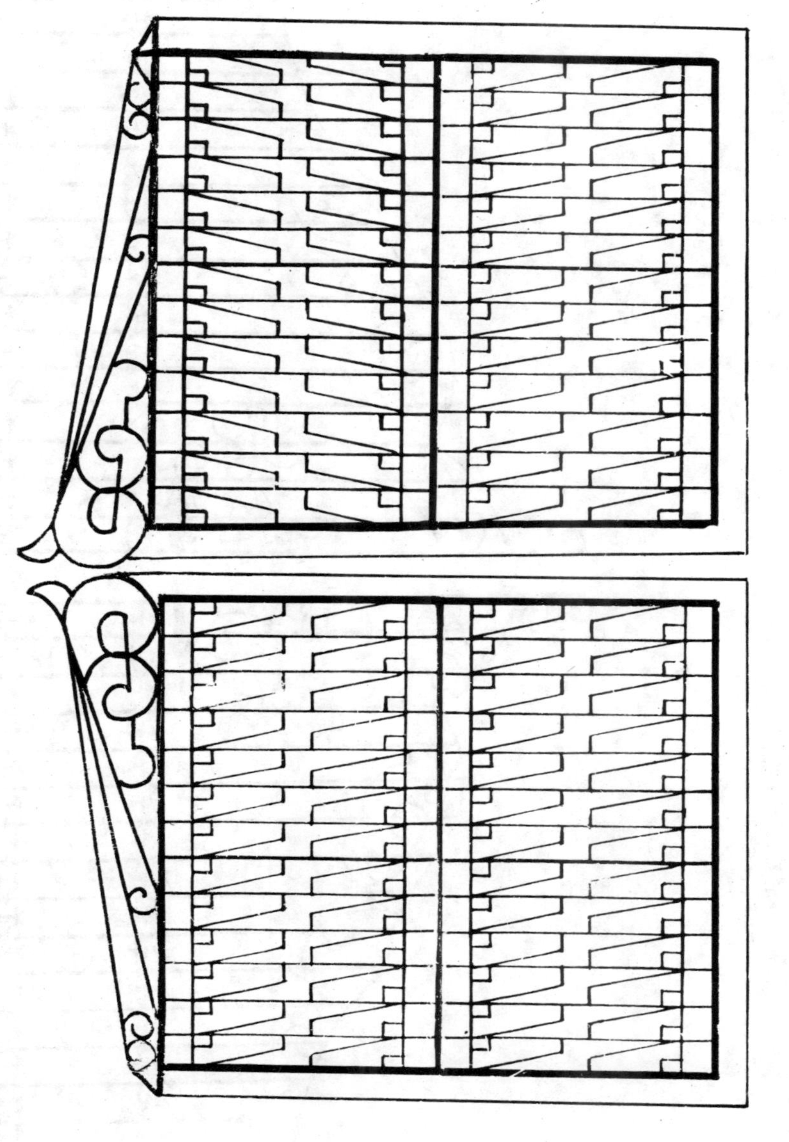

Architectural design suitable for Small and Big Factories.

Most attractive fine art design in wrought iron bars construction

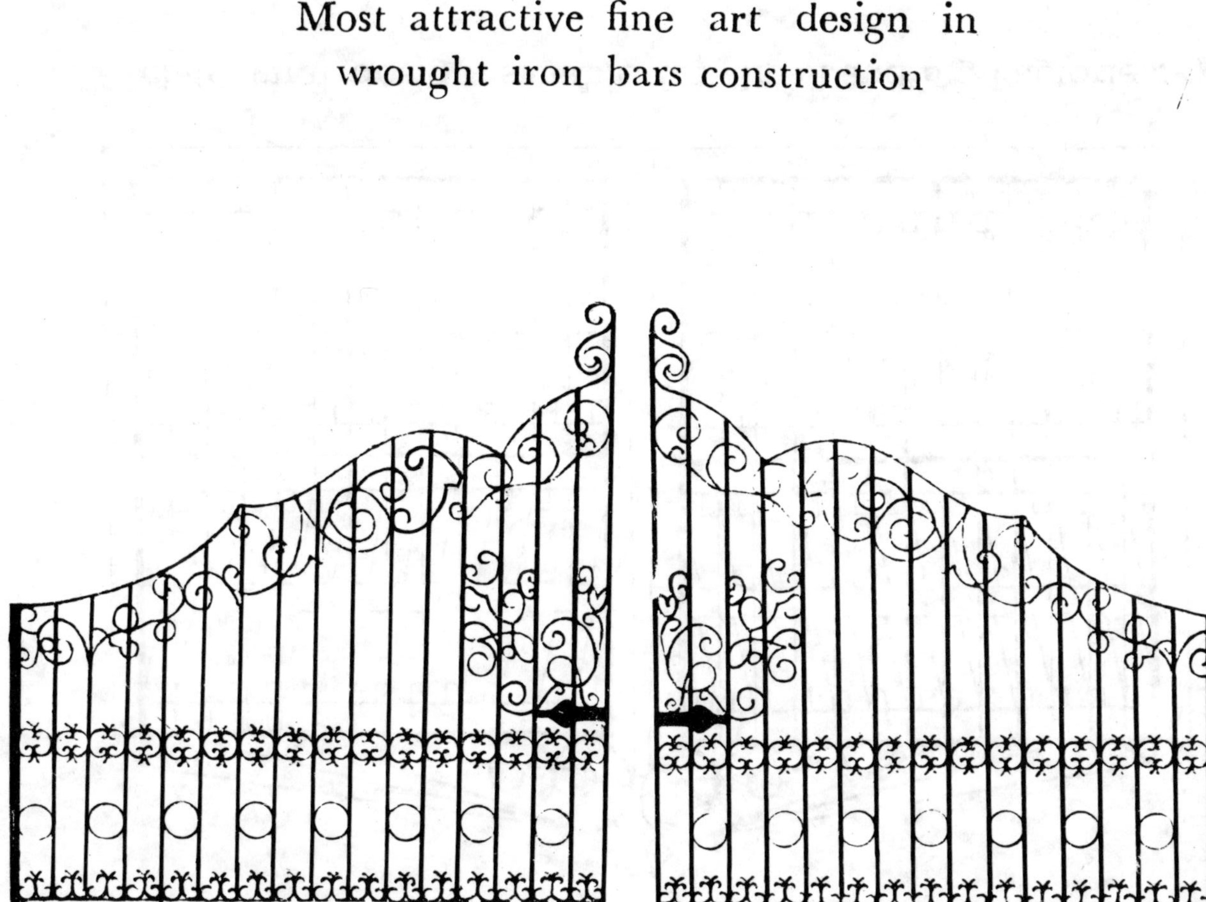

Complete Ancient Design gives an idea and Art of Mughal Period Designs

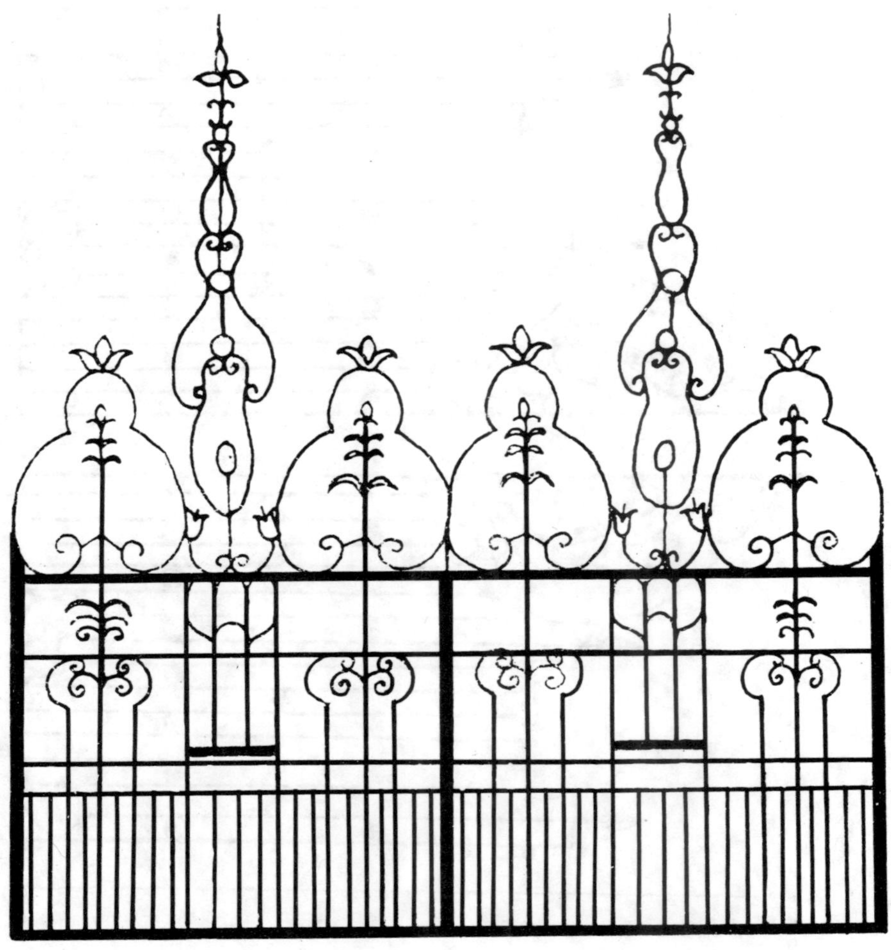

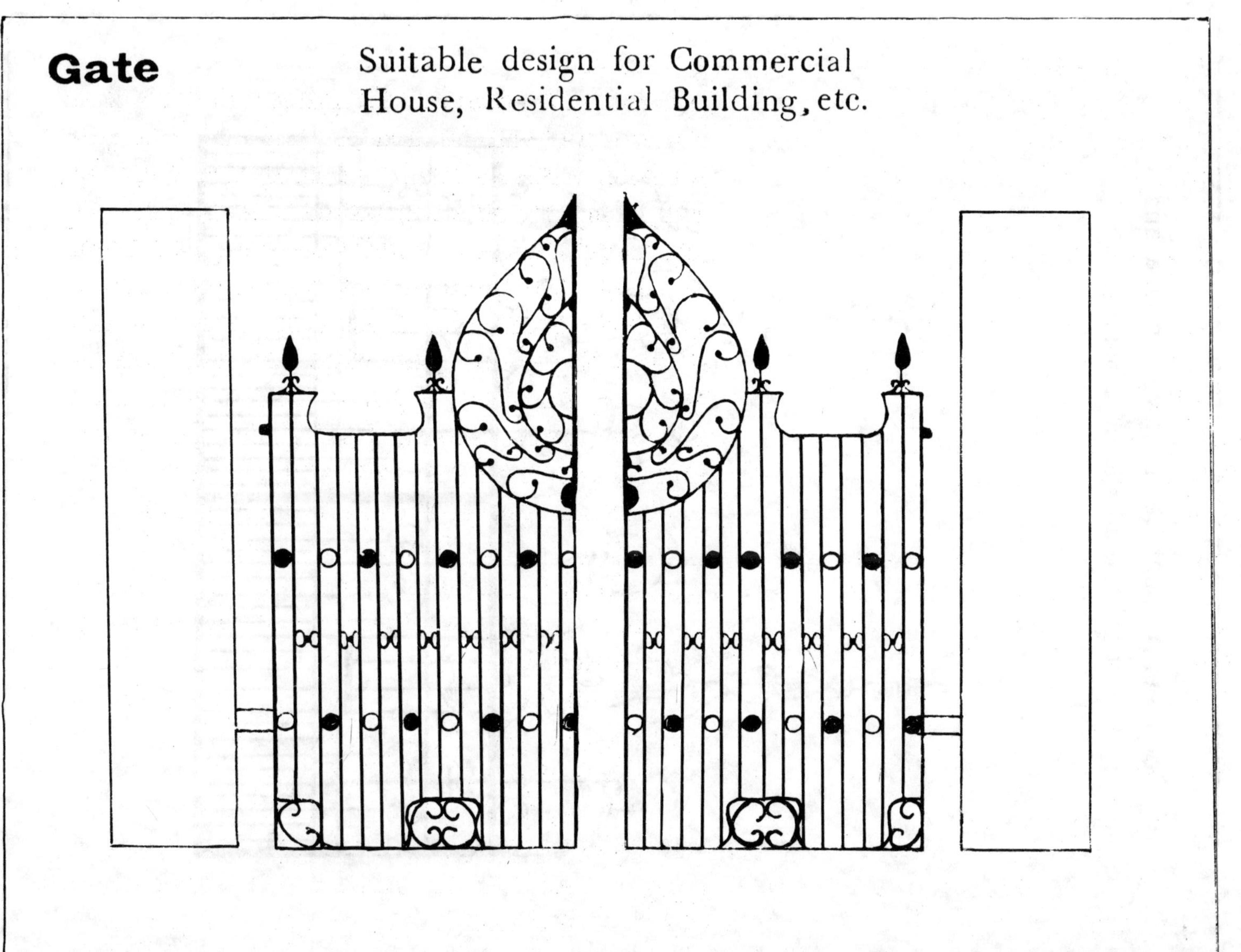
Gate
Suitable design for Commercial
House, Residential Building, etc.

A beatiful Indian ancient design of modern Art.

Attractive designs of small and big circles.
For strong construction.

Ultra-modern designs of solid rod welded in Geometrical principle.

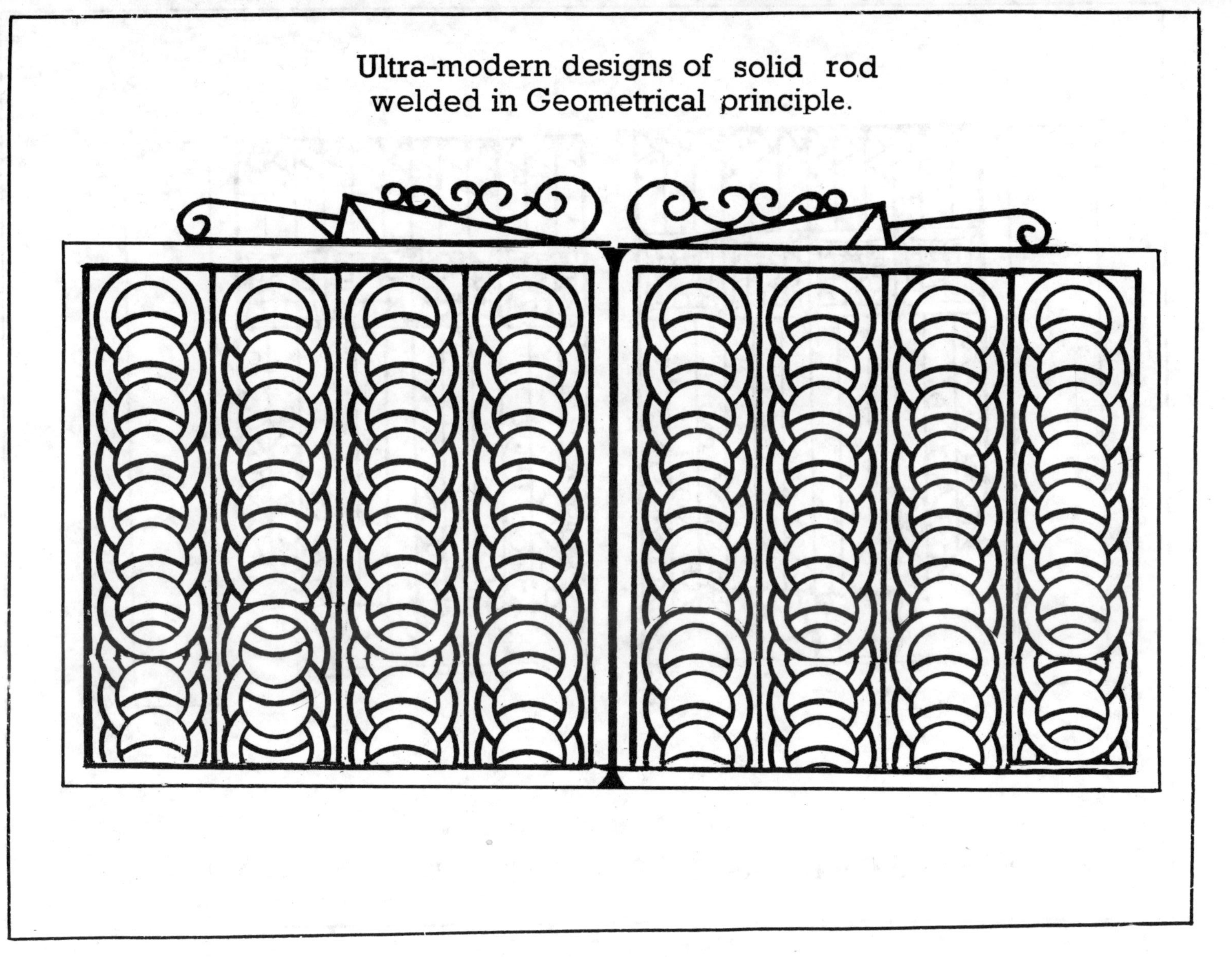

A Common design of Gates for Small and Big Factories.

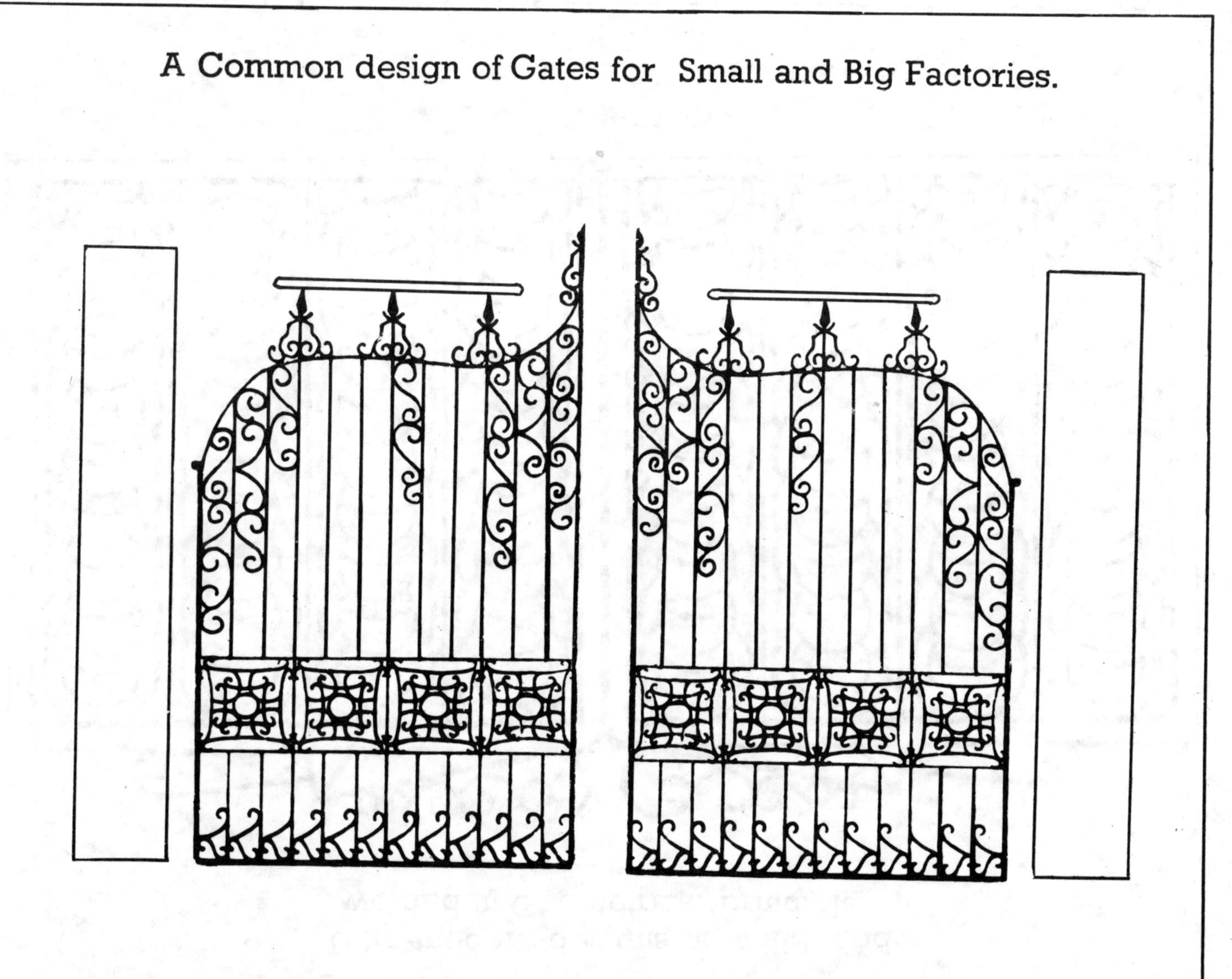

Design of Stars welded and inserted with solid Iron bars

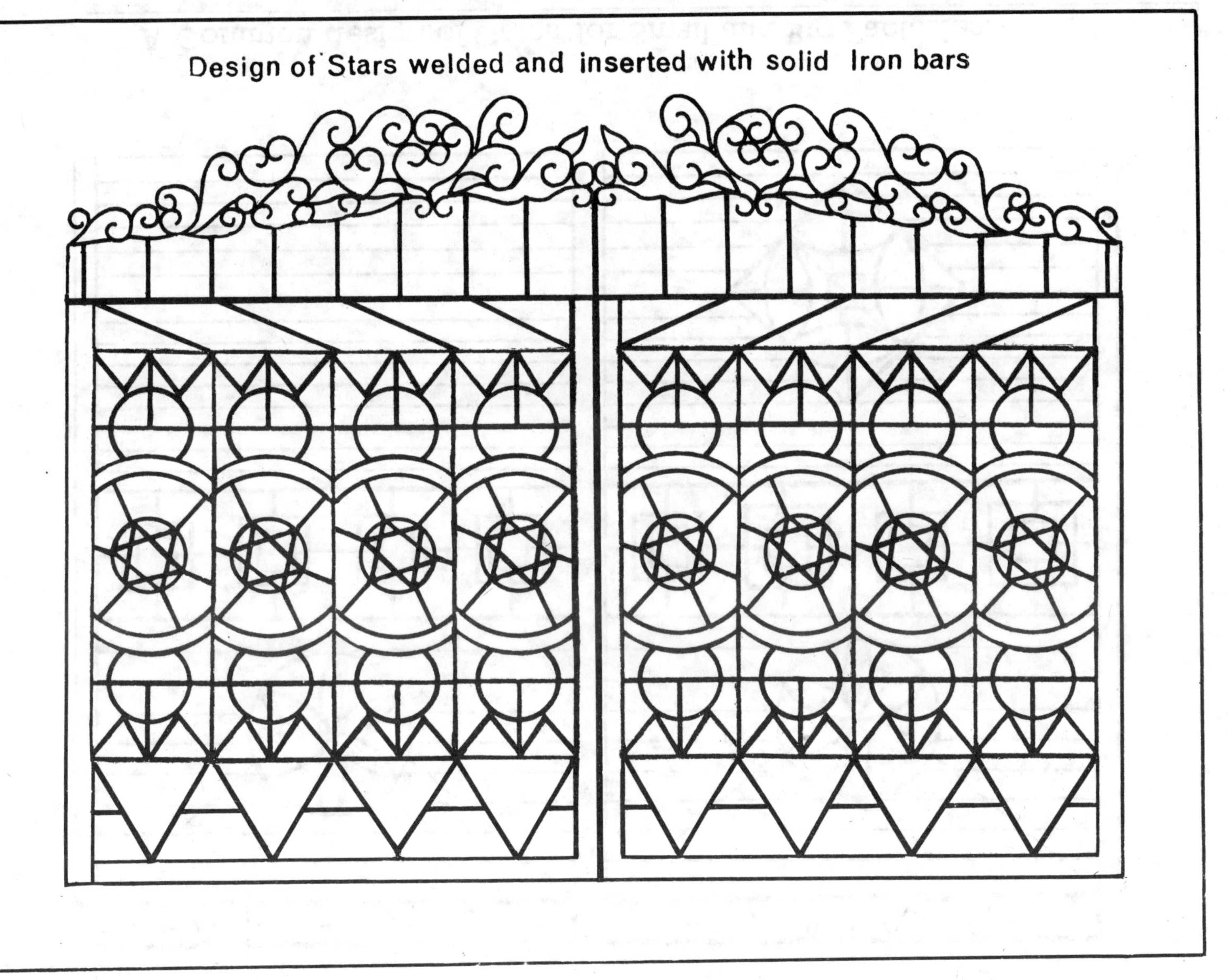

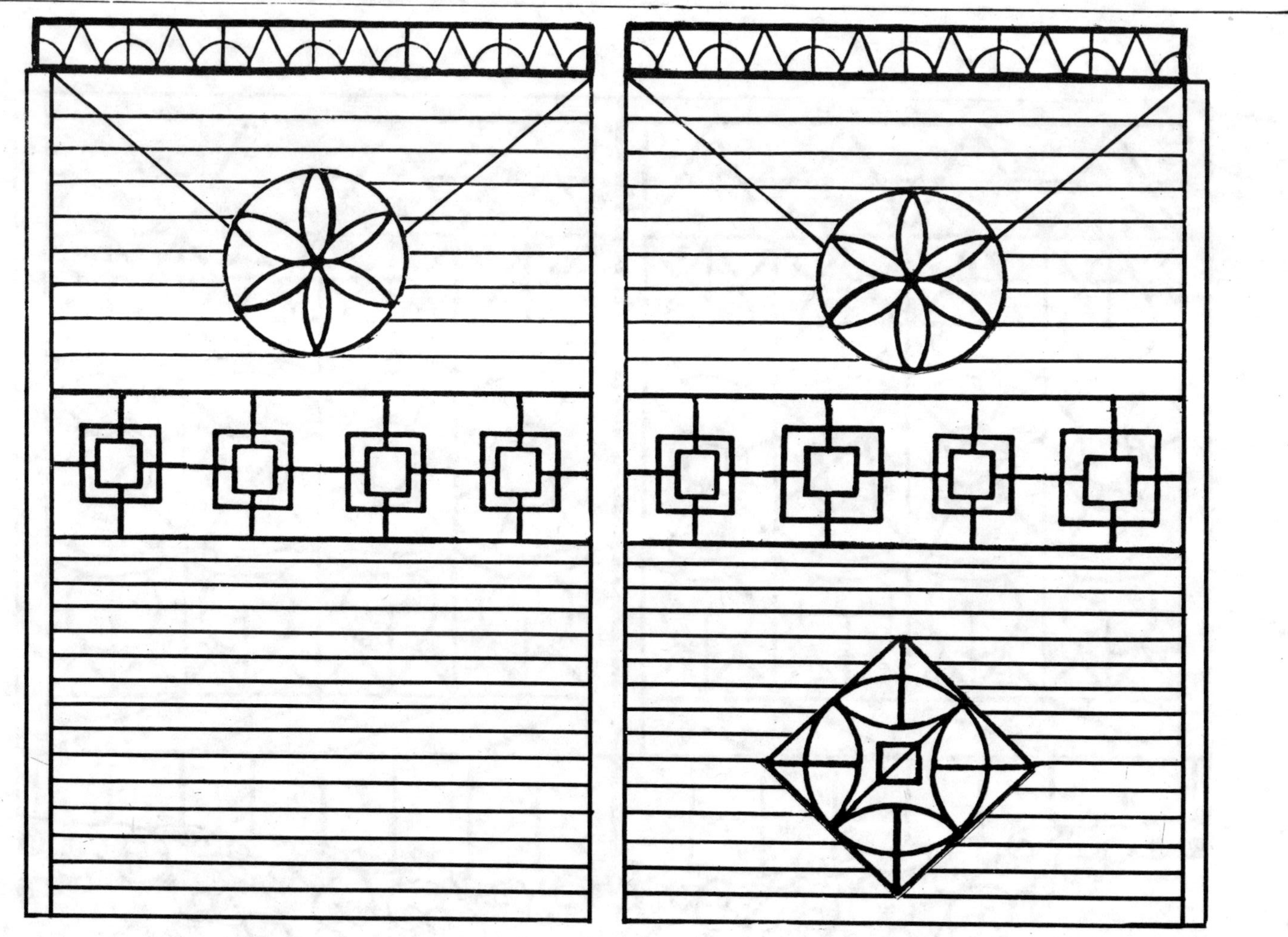

A Common design of Gates for Small and Big Factories.

Quite Modern Big Gate design of solid Iron bars for Newly Constructed House.

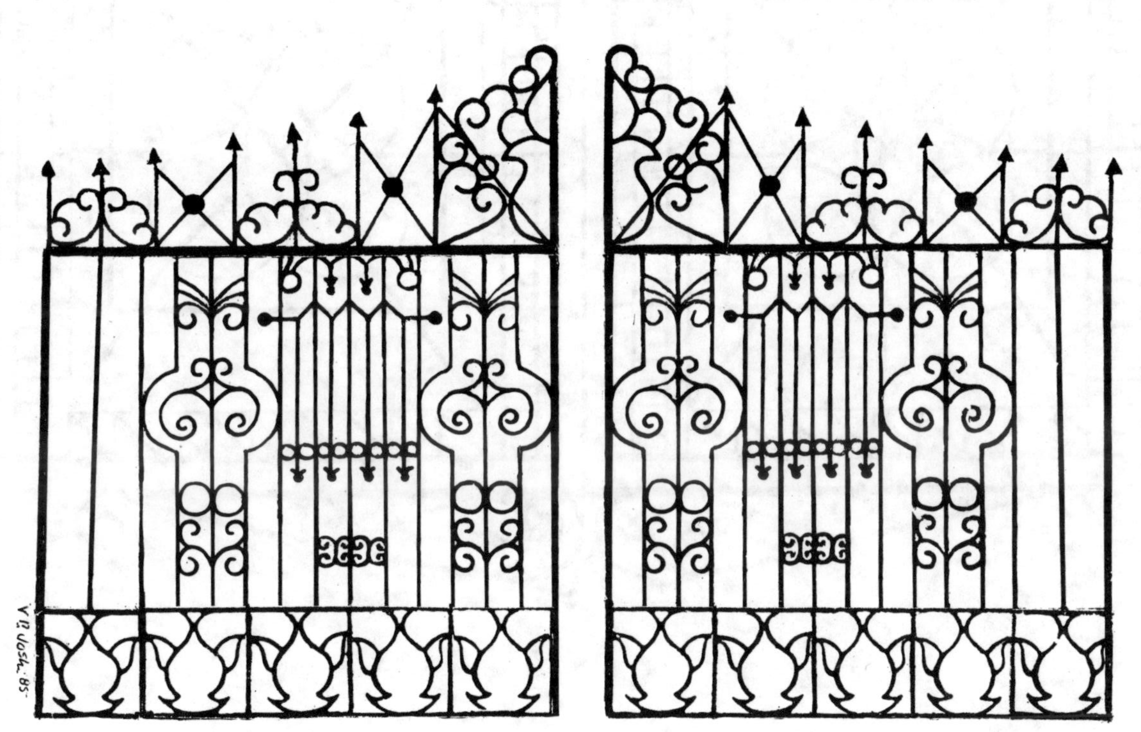

designs of Grill with modern and fine art touch.

Switzerland design of modern Grill

Ultra-modern designs of Japan.
Made of thick and thin solid

V B Joshi '85

Beautiful Railing

Thick and thin vertical Iron bar Designs

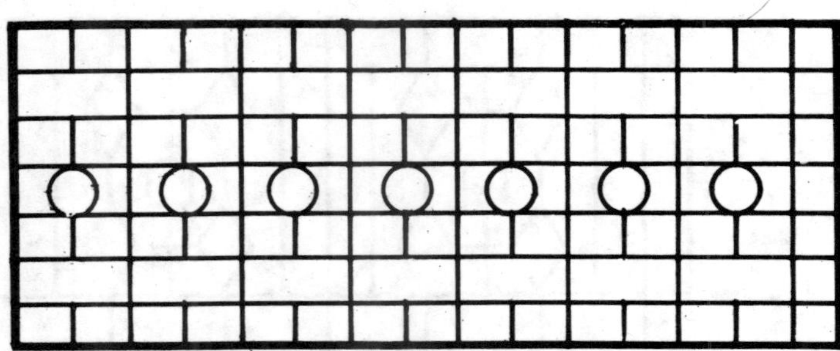

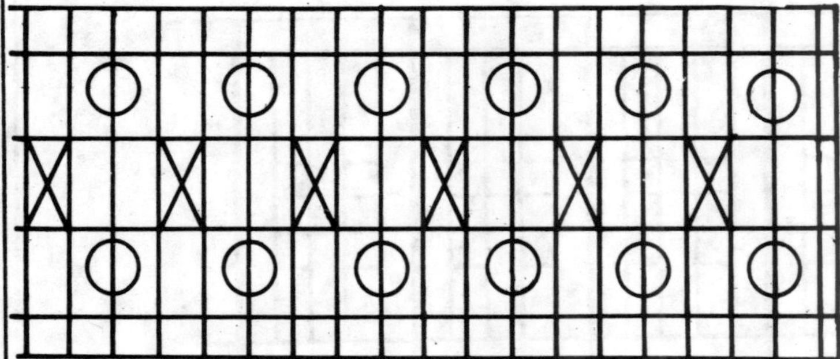

wrought Iron bars crossings Design.

Ancient Art. design of Scotland

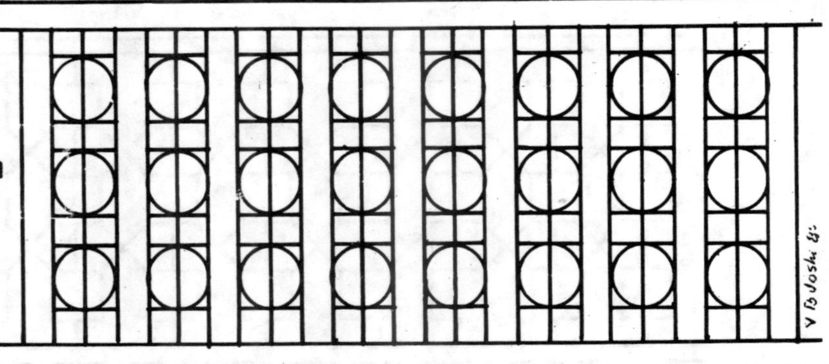

Design of Square M.S. Bars

Design of Vertical Iron Bars

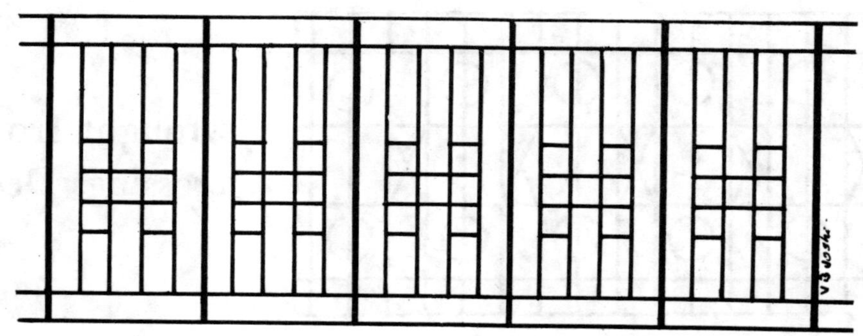

American design for Artistic Building.

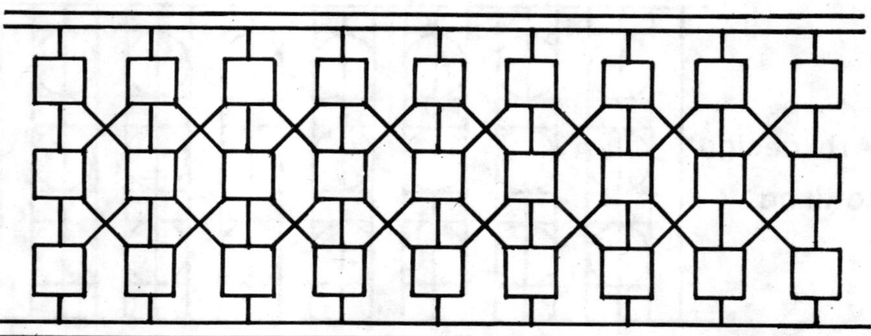

Symmetrical setting of

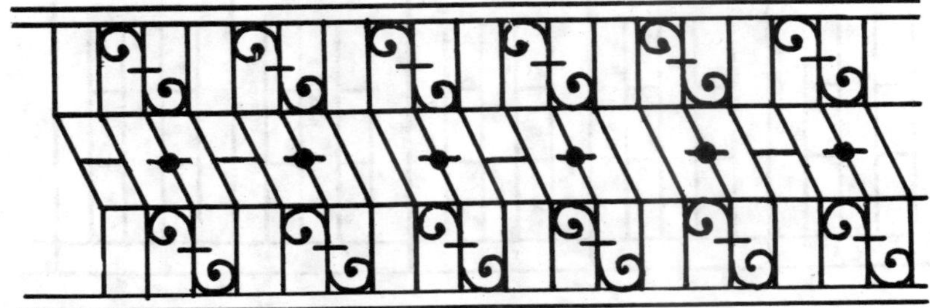

Semicircle and

straight Iron bars

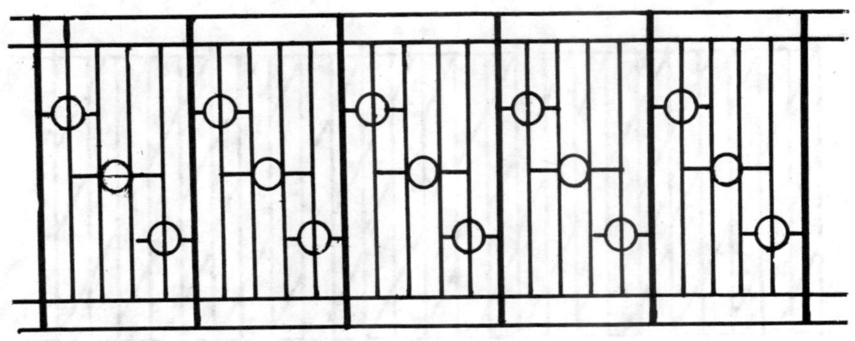

Artistic Design of Cast Iron Rods

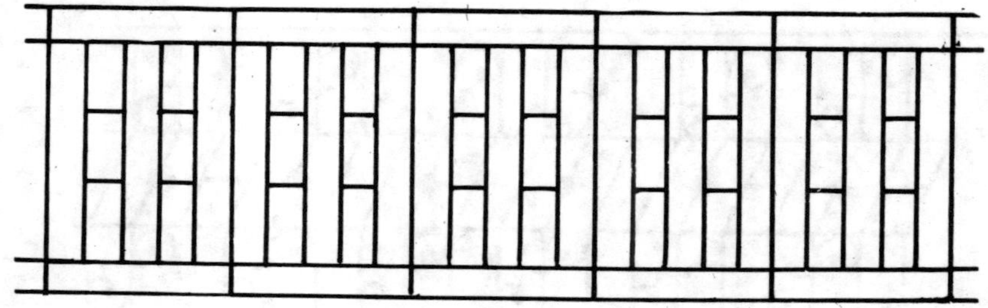

Ancient Design of Grills increases the

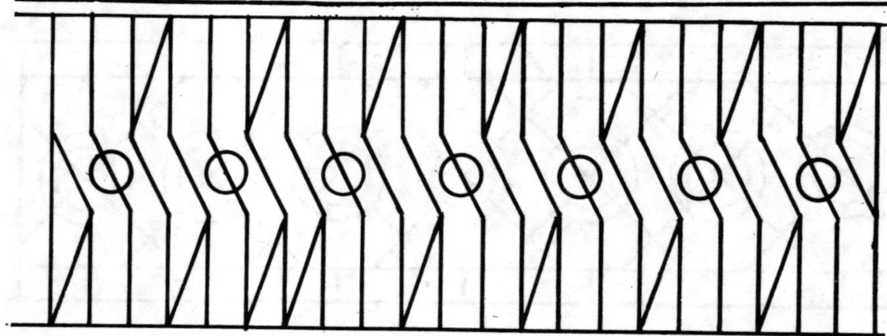

beauty of Small or Big Building.

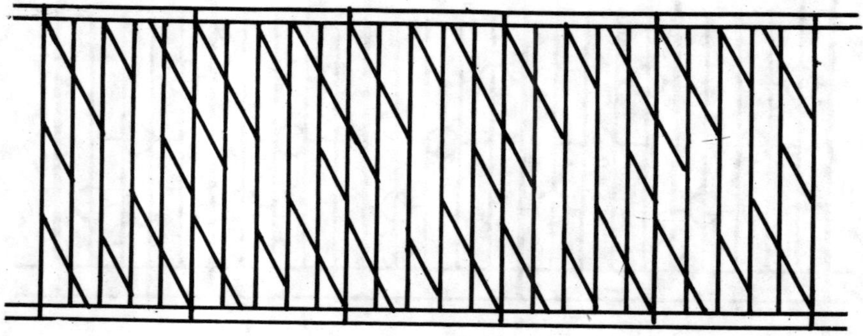

An interesting penetrated design for

modern construction and decoration

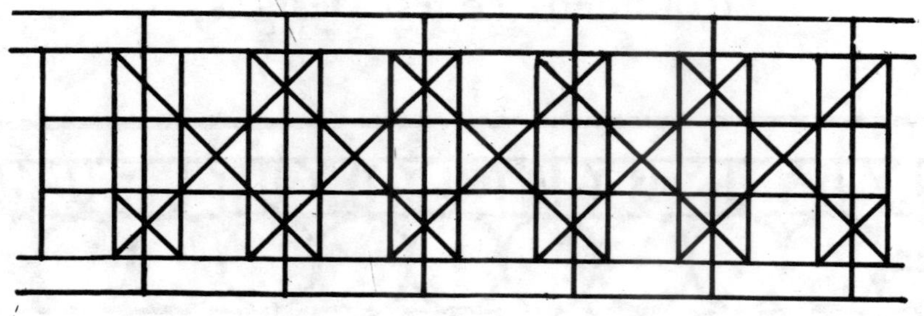

Most Practical U.K. design

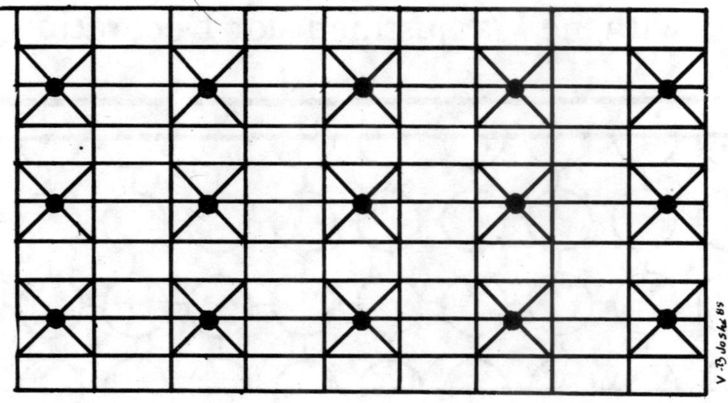

Good design of penetrated Iron bars

Rounded edges Designs,

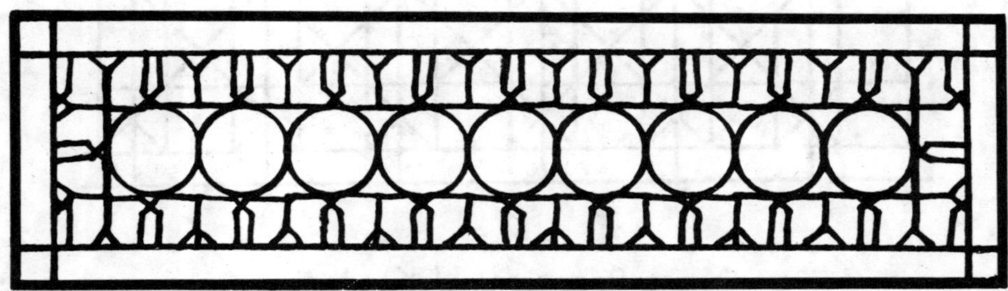

with new adjustment for Decoration.

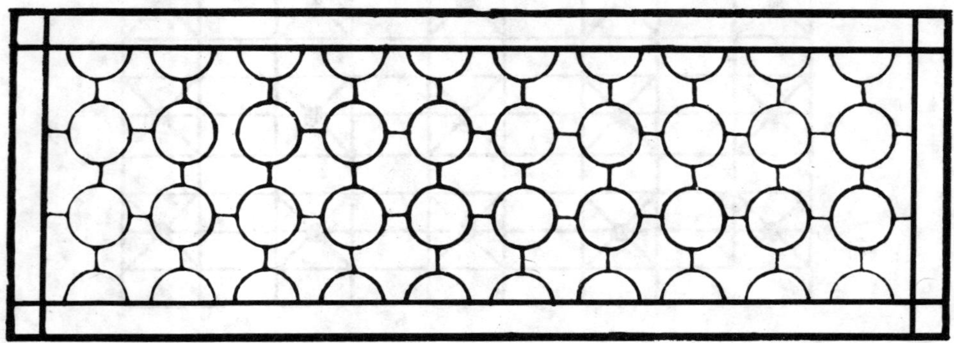

New designs of Curved solid Iron bars

Round Iron bar designs in layer

style, welded on the frames

West Germany's design

for biggest construction.

Beautiful Japanese design.

Strong and Best design of
Railing for Long Construction.

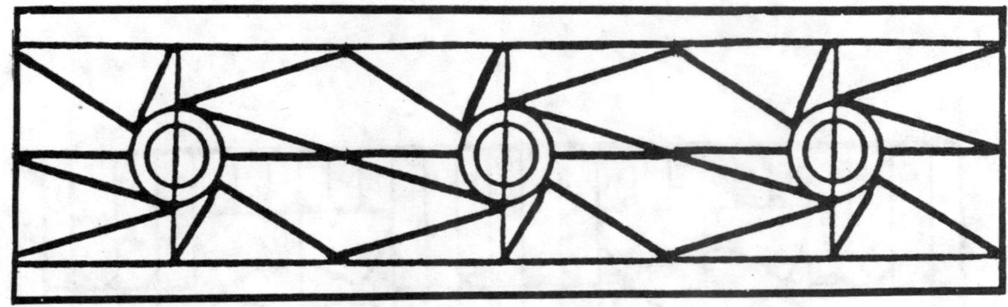

New pattern of straight and Round

M.S. Iron Bar designs.

Ancient Design of Grills increases the beauty of Small or Big Building.

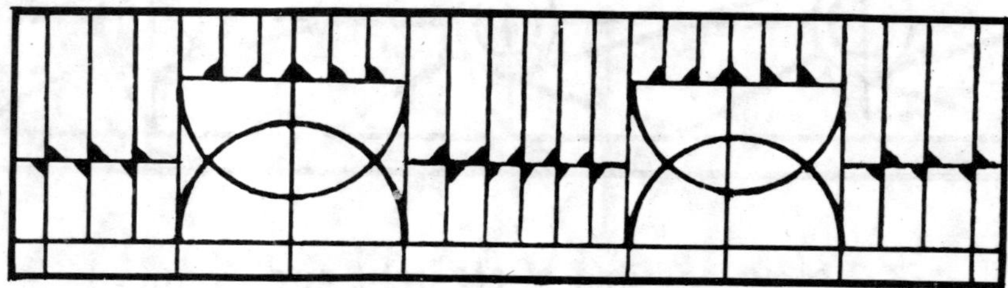

Square and flate Steel Bars design

Quite Suitable design for Cinema buildings etc.

Beautiful Railing

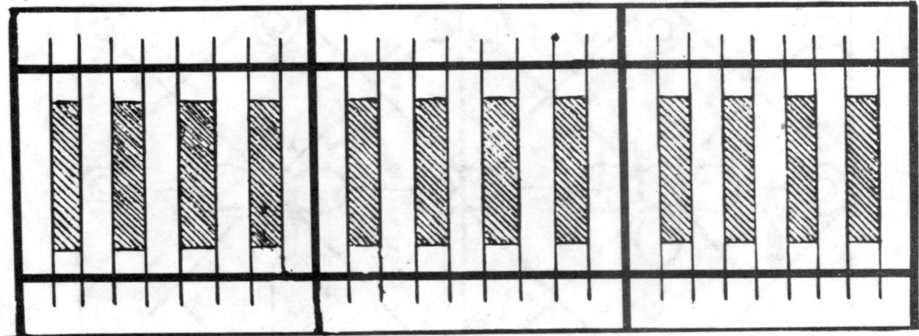

Architectural design of solid Square bar frame.

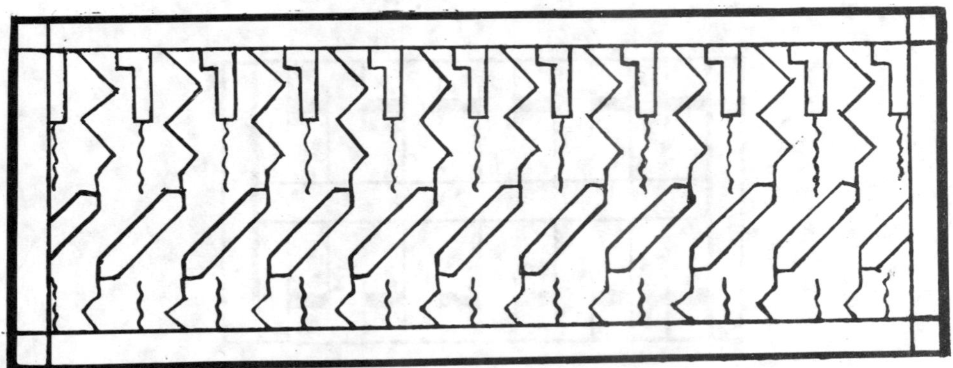

Complete Ancient Design gives an idea and Art of Mughal Period construction.

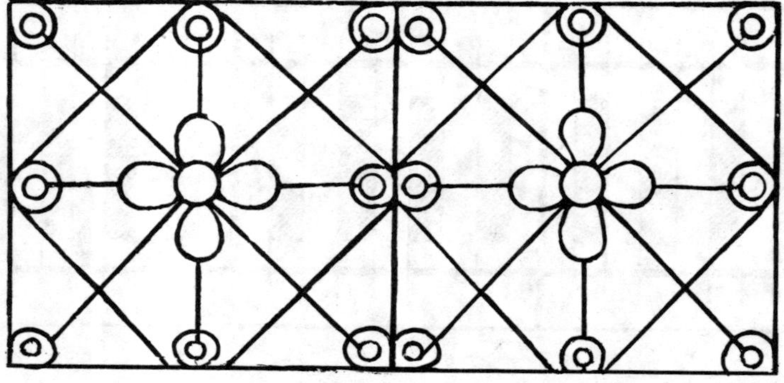

A Common design of

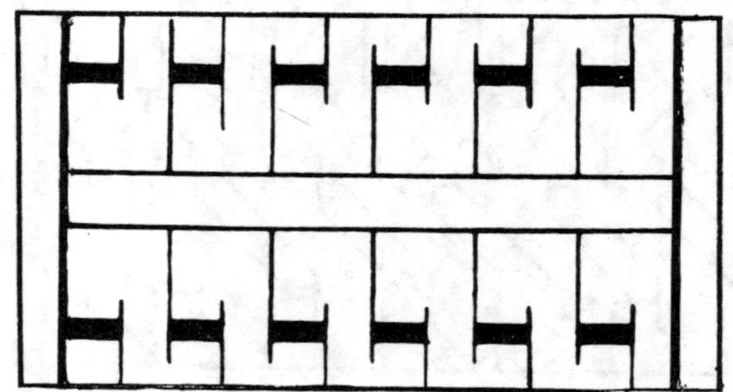

Round Iron bar designs in layer
style, welded on the frames

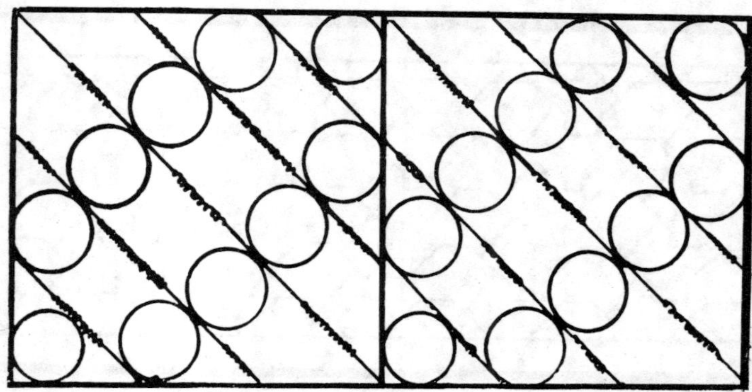

Very simple and beautiful design of Tokyo.

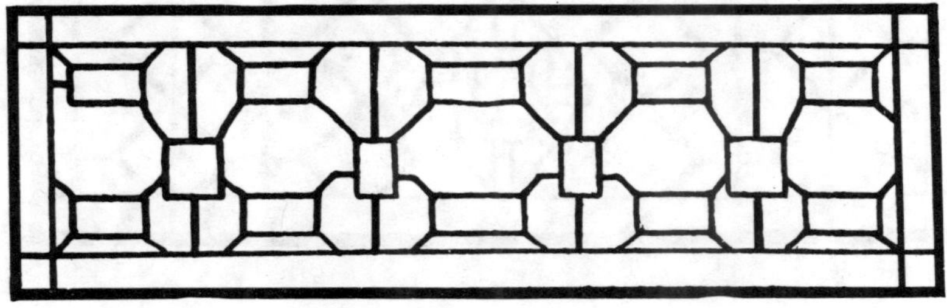

Very strong designs for

decoration of residential and commercial building.

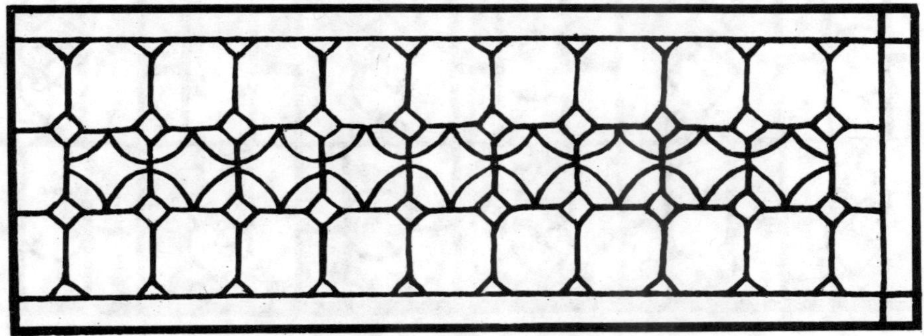

Quite suitable German design for new Building.

Flowery design of wrought Iron bars,

Indian design with modern arrangaments.

Architectural Designs of Staircases

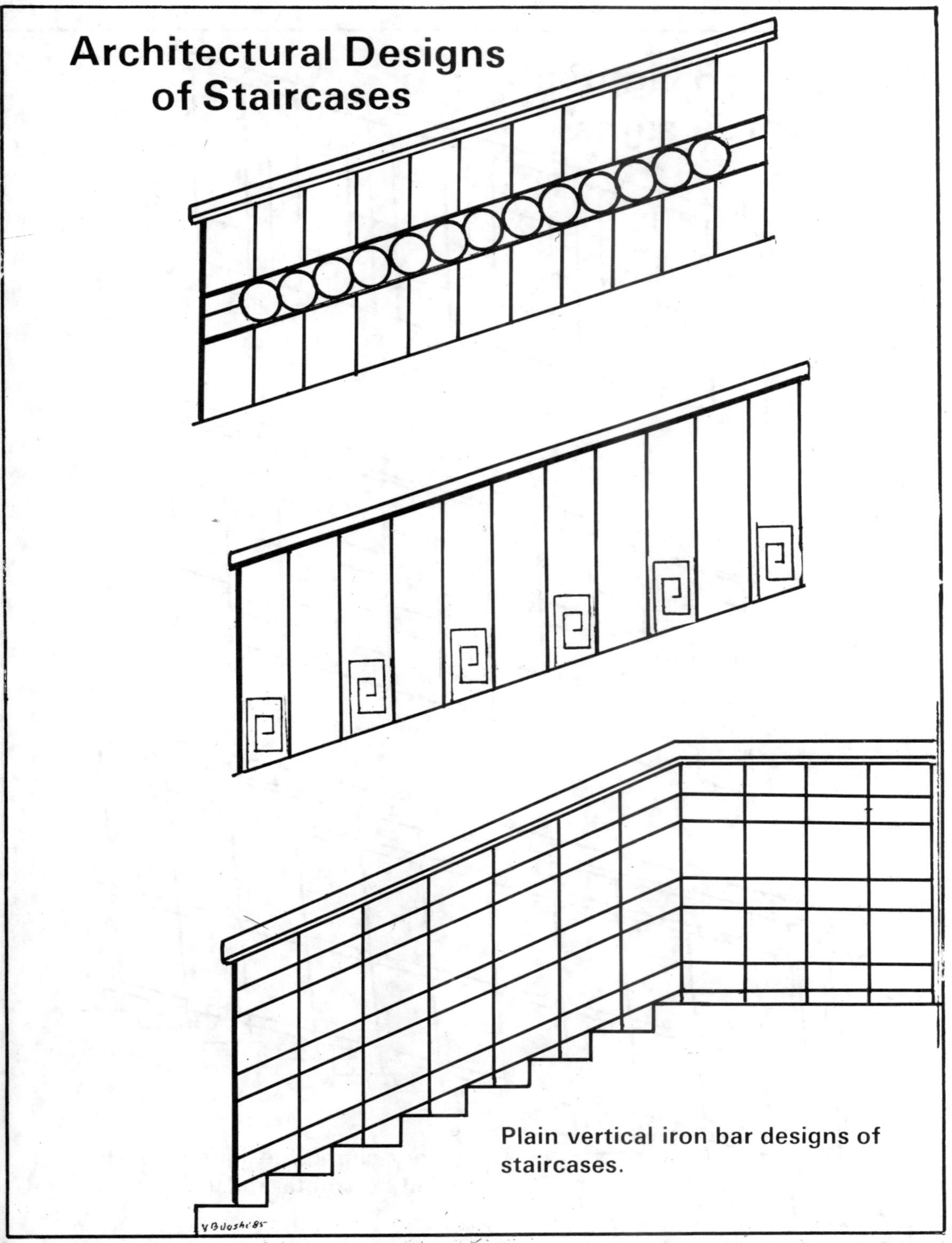

Plain vertical iron bar designs of staircases.

Simple and Light in Weight Designs

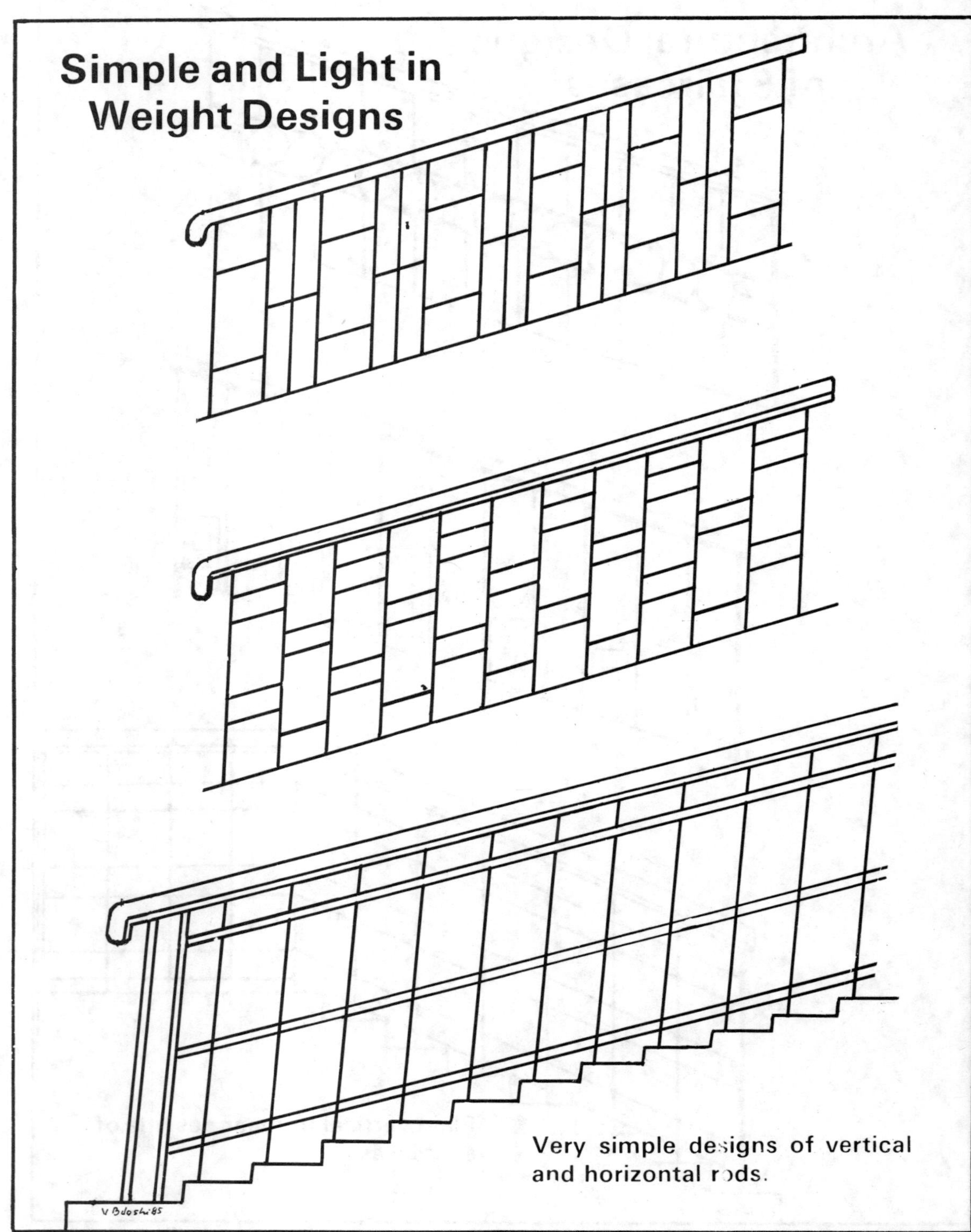

Very simple designs of vertical and horizontal rods.

Architectural Designs

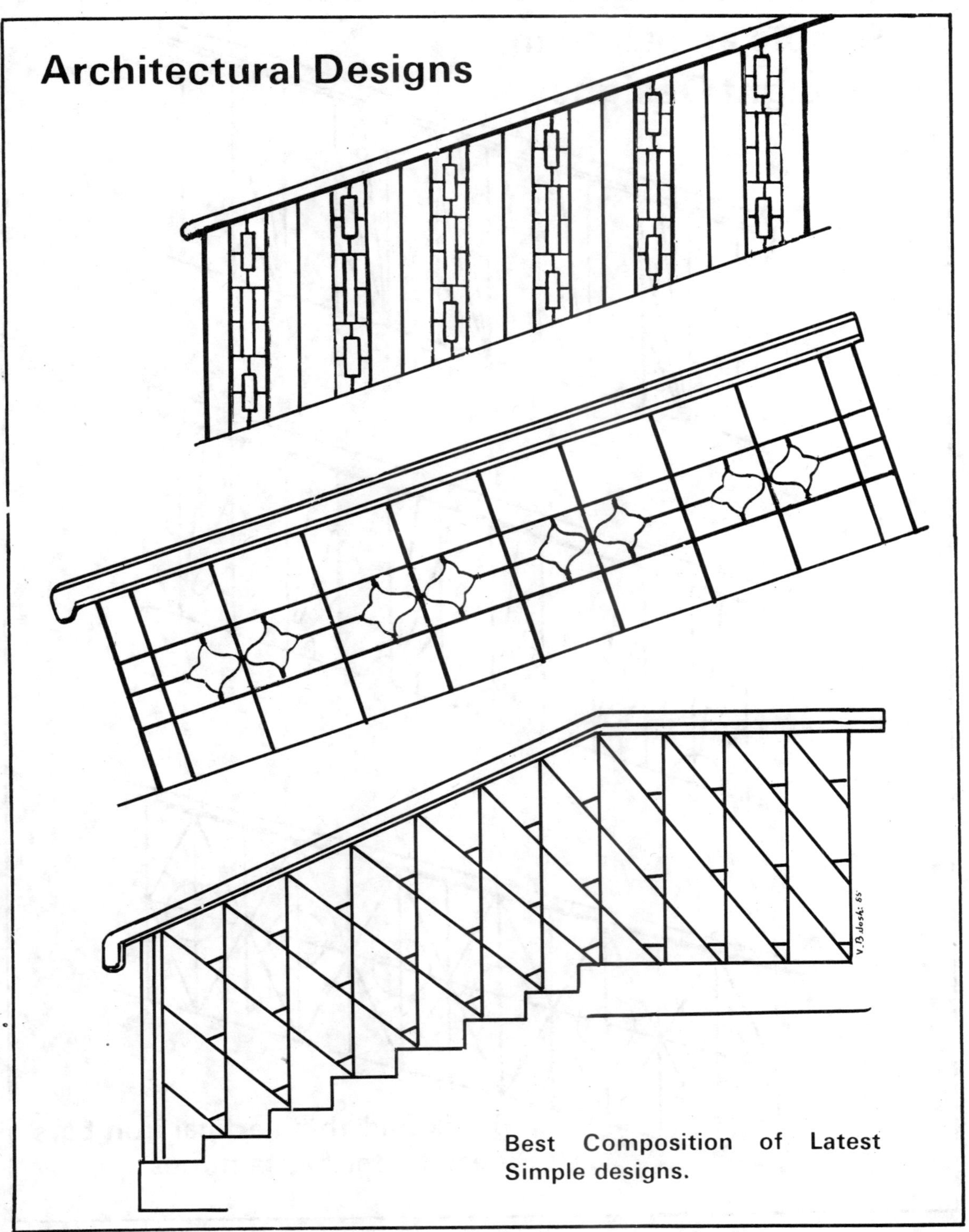

Best Composition of Latest Simple designs.

Simple and Light in Weight Designs

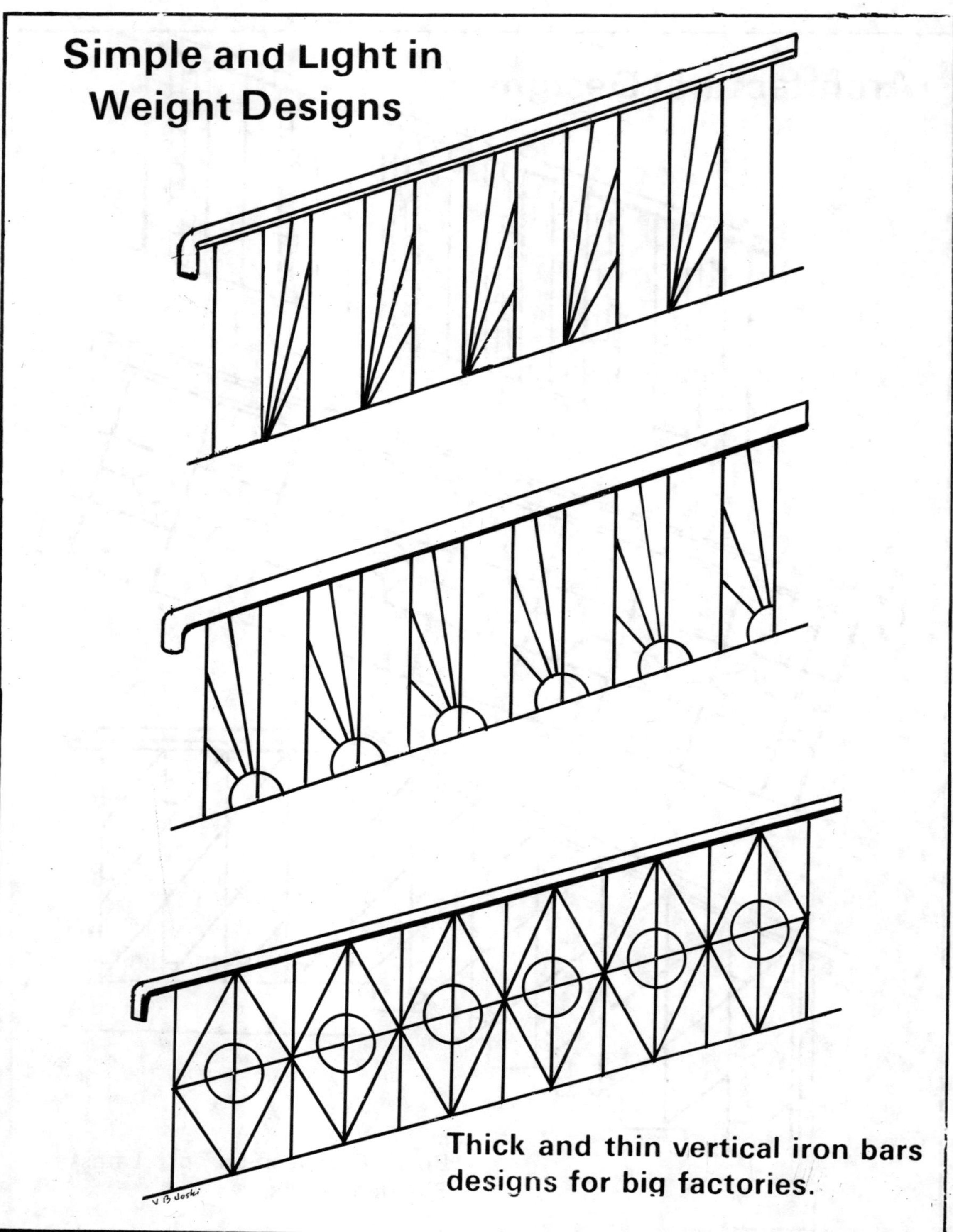

Thick and thin vertical iron bars designs for big factories.

Simple and Light Designs

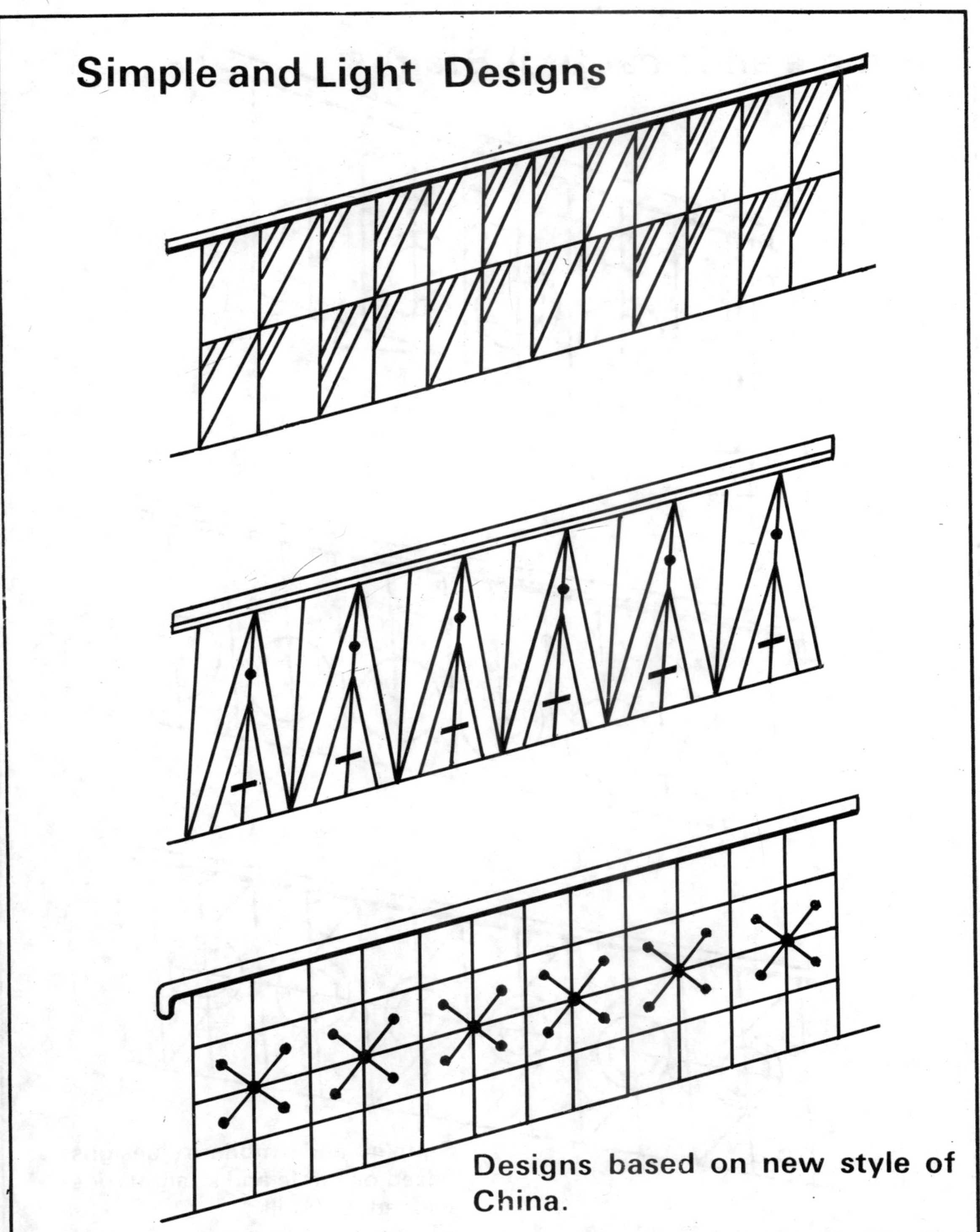

Designs based on new style of China.

Simple and Beautiful Stairs

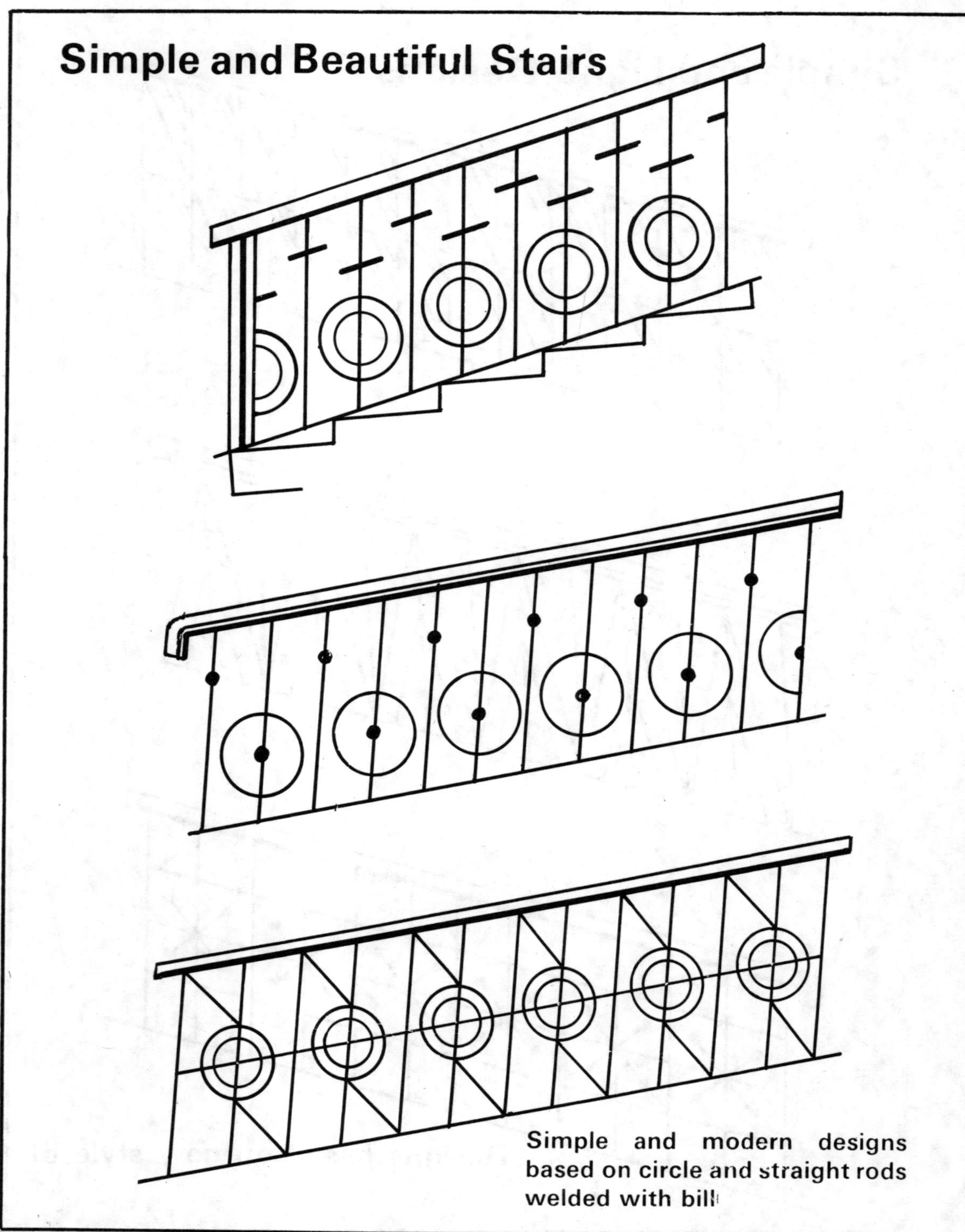

Simple and modern designs based on circle and straight rods welded with bill

Modern Designs

Best Tokyo's designs arranged in symmetrical pattern.

Beautiful Stairs

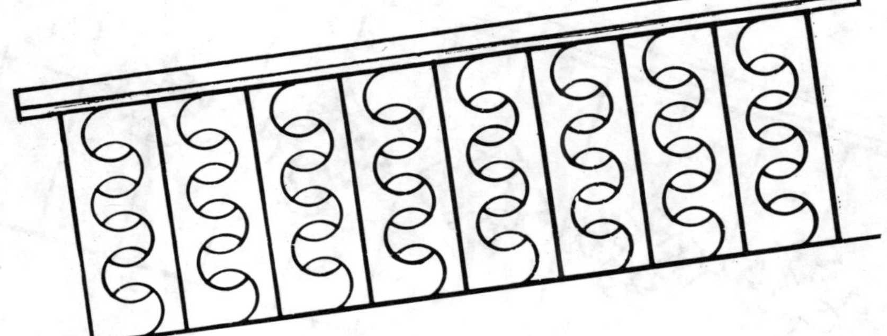

Flowery designs constructed in circular pattern, welded with bended rods.

Geometrical Designs

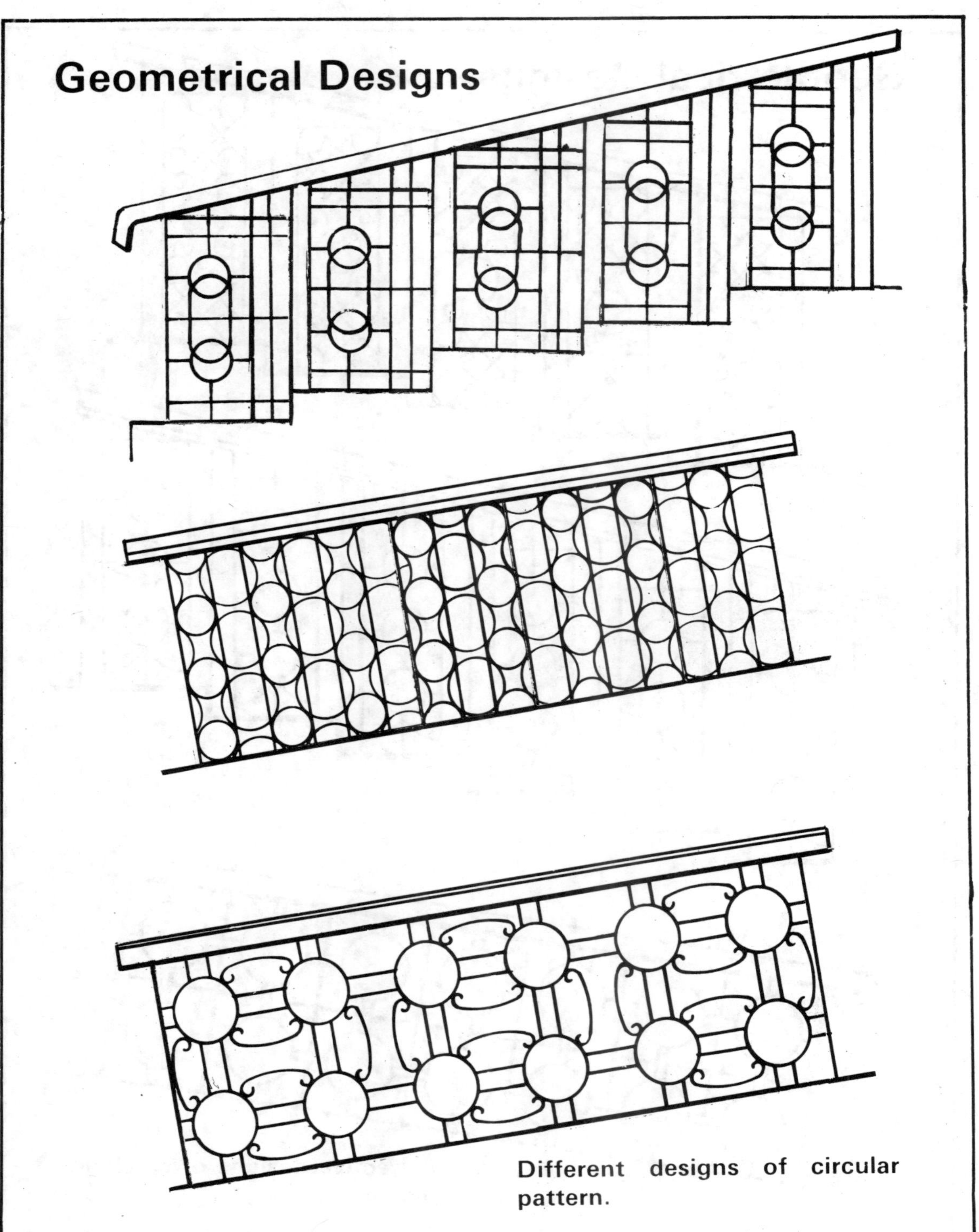

Different designs of circular pattern.

Geometrical Designs

Attractive designs of small and big circles.

Geometrical Designs of Staircases

Intermixing designs of circle and straight rods.

Ultra Modern Designs of Staircases

Modern designs of straight rods, circles and rectangles arranged in architectural style.

Ultra Modern Designs of Staircases

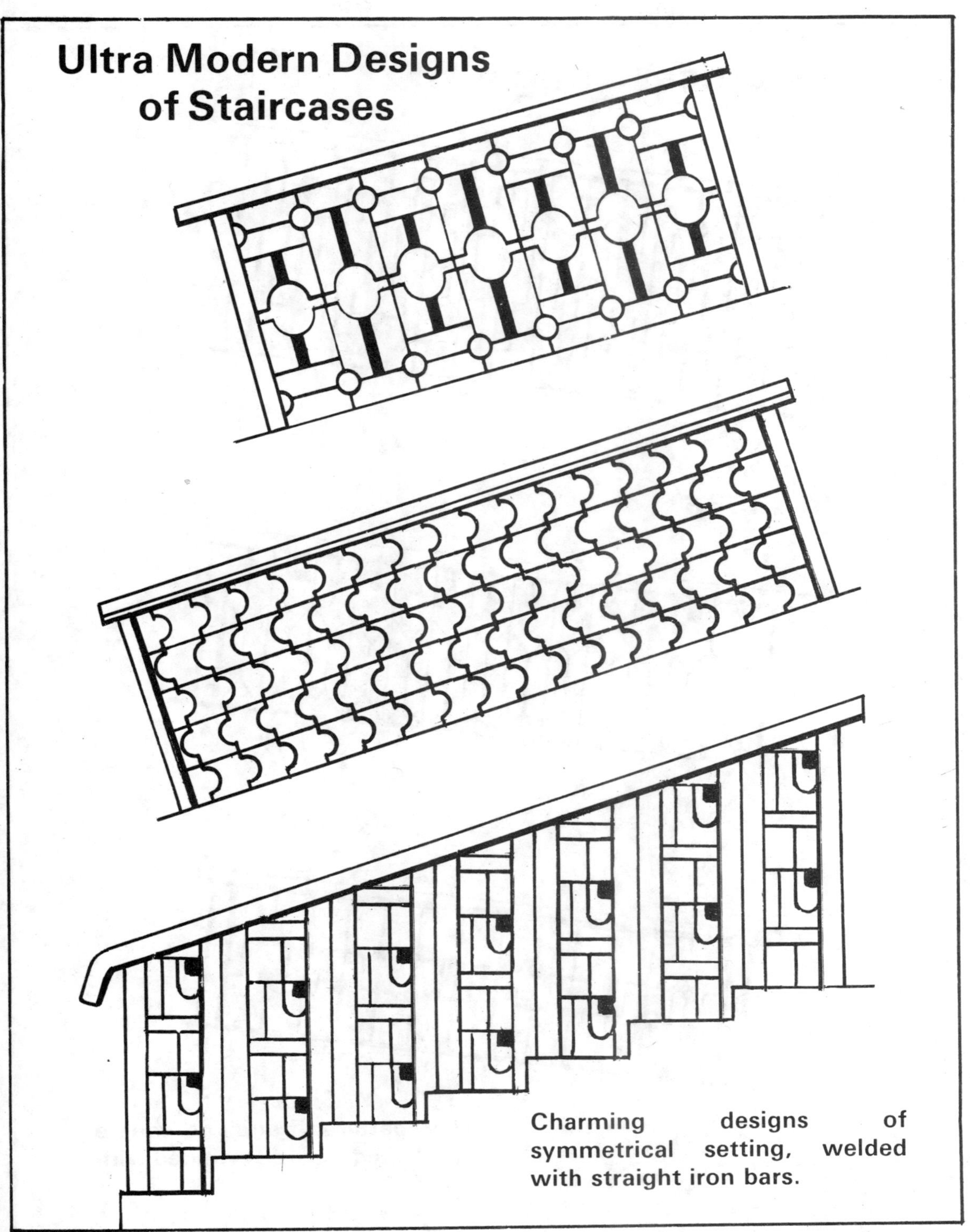

Charming designs of symmetrical setting, welded with straight iron bars.

Geometrical Designs of

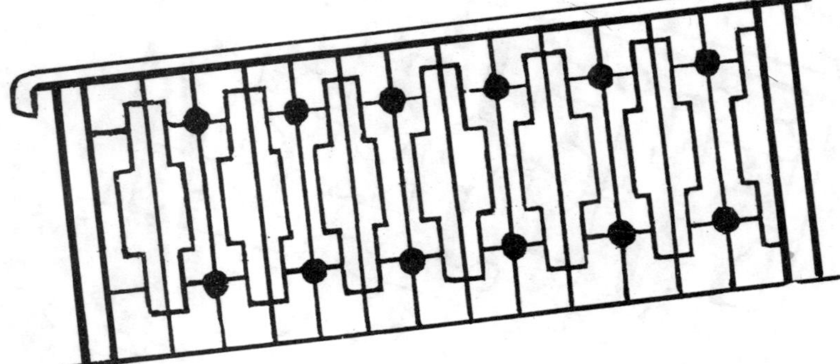

Staircases

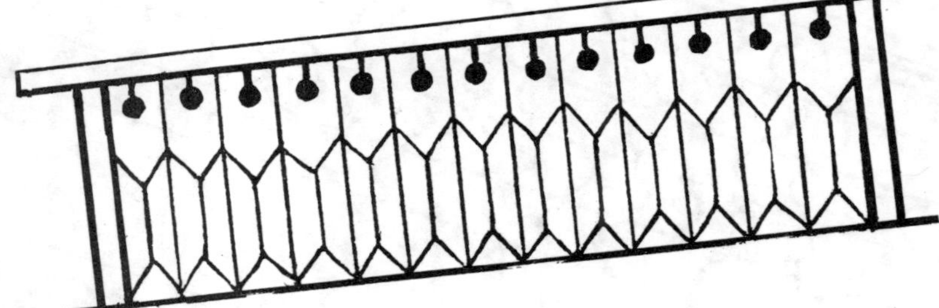

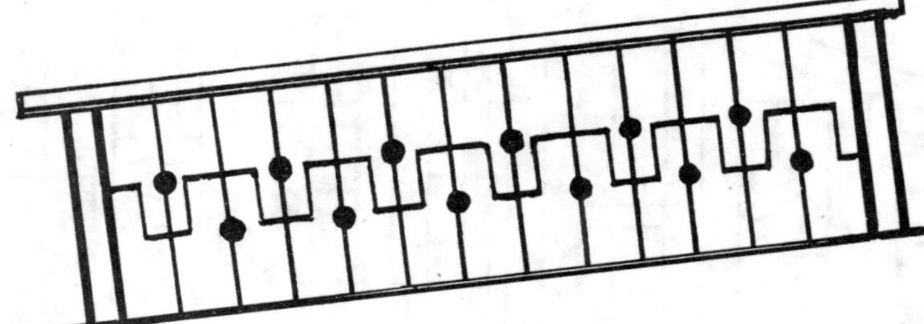

New pattern of straight, square and hexagonal rods welded with billas.

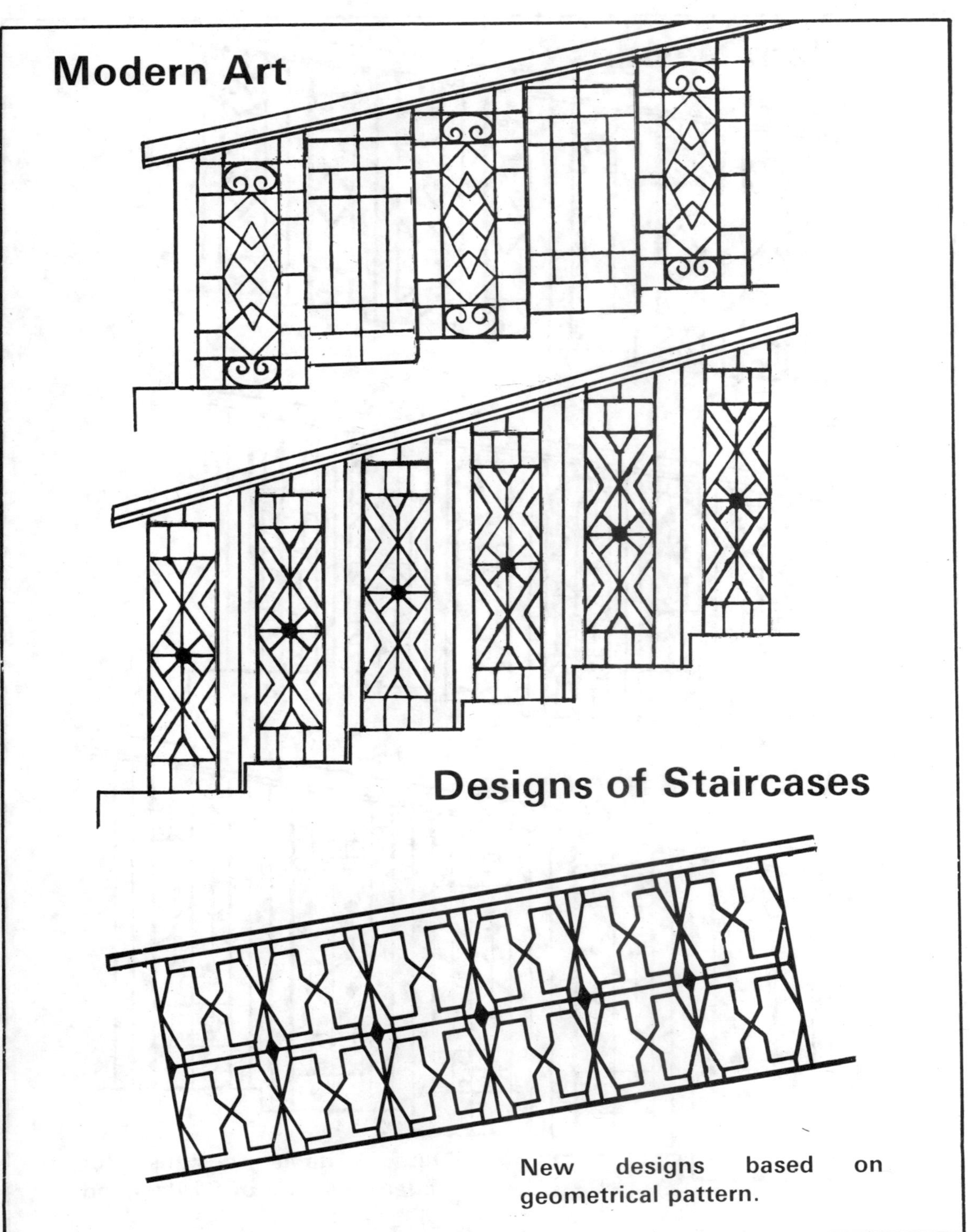
Modern Art
Designs of Staircases
New designs based on geometrical pattern.

Modern Designs

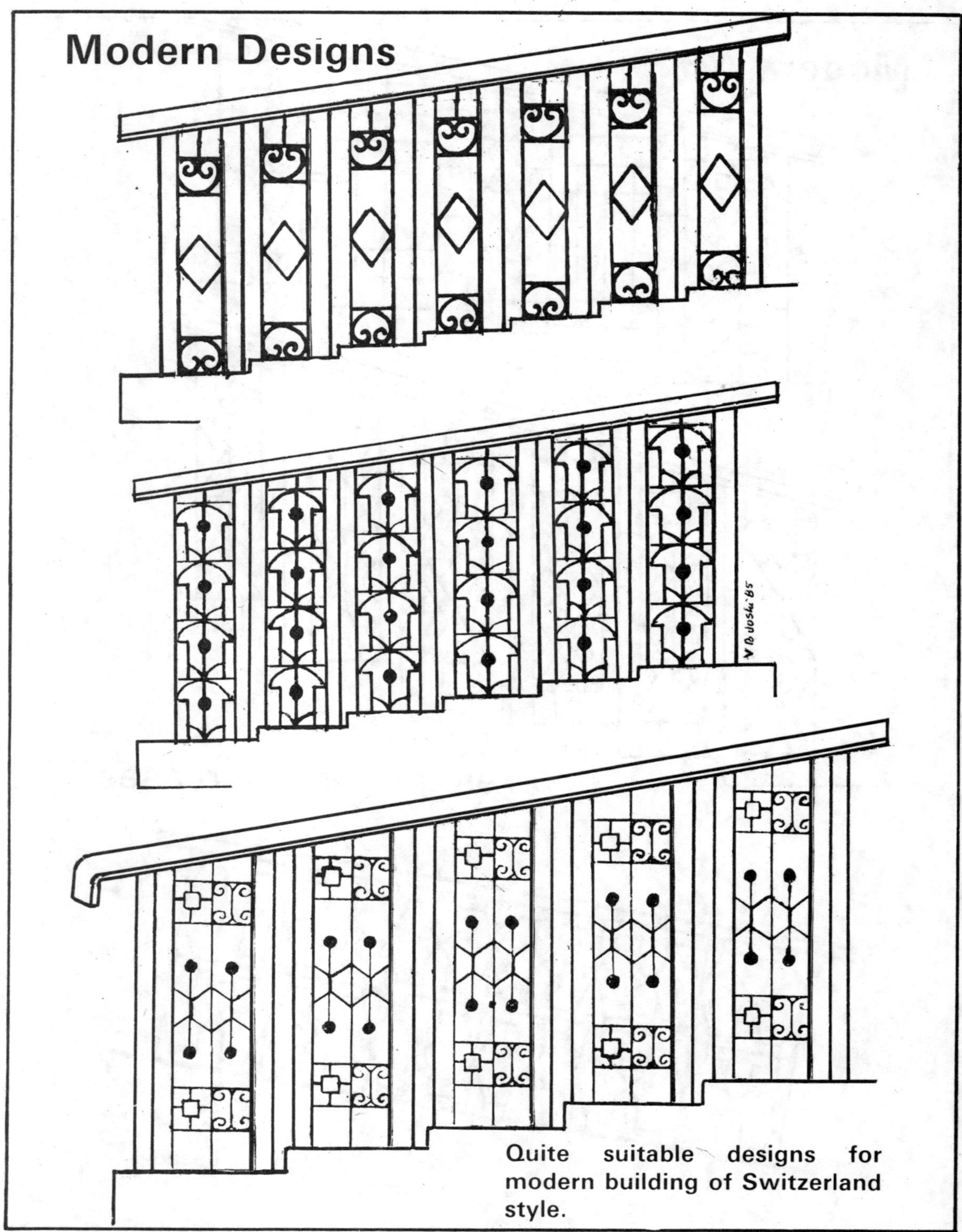

Quite suitable designs for modern building of Switzerland style.

Modern Art Designs

Staircases

Ancient designs of staircases grills welded in modern style.

Architectural Designs of
Staircases
Square and flat rods designs of
U.K.
V.B Joshi 85

Architectural Designs

Very strong designs of solid straight rods, with billas.

Latest Designs of Staircases

Symmetrical setting of square and round rods designs bended in leaves pattern.

Latest Designs of Staircases

A composition of best and latest designs of ultra modern style.

Latest Designs of Staircases

Best Japanese designs of M.S. bars.

Latest Designs of Staircases

Artistic designs of cast iron bars decorated with billas.

Modern Designs

Most artistic designs in flower pattern.

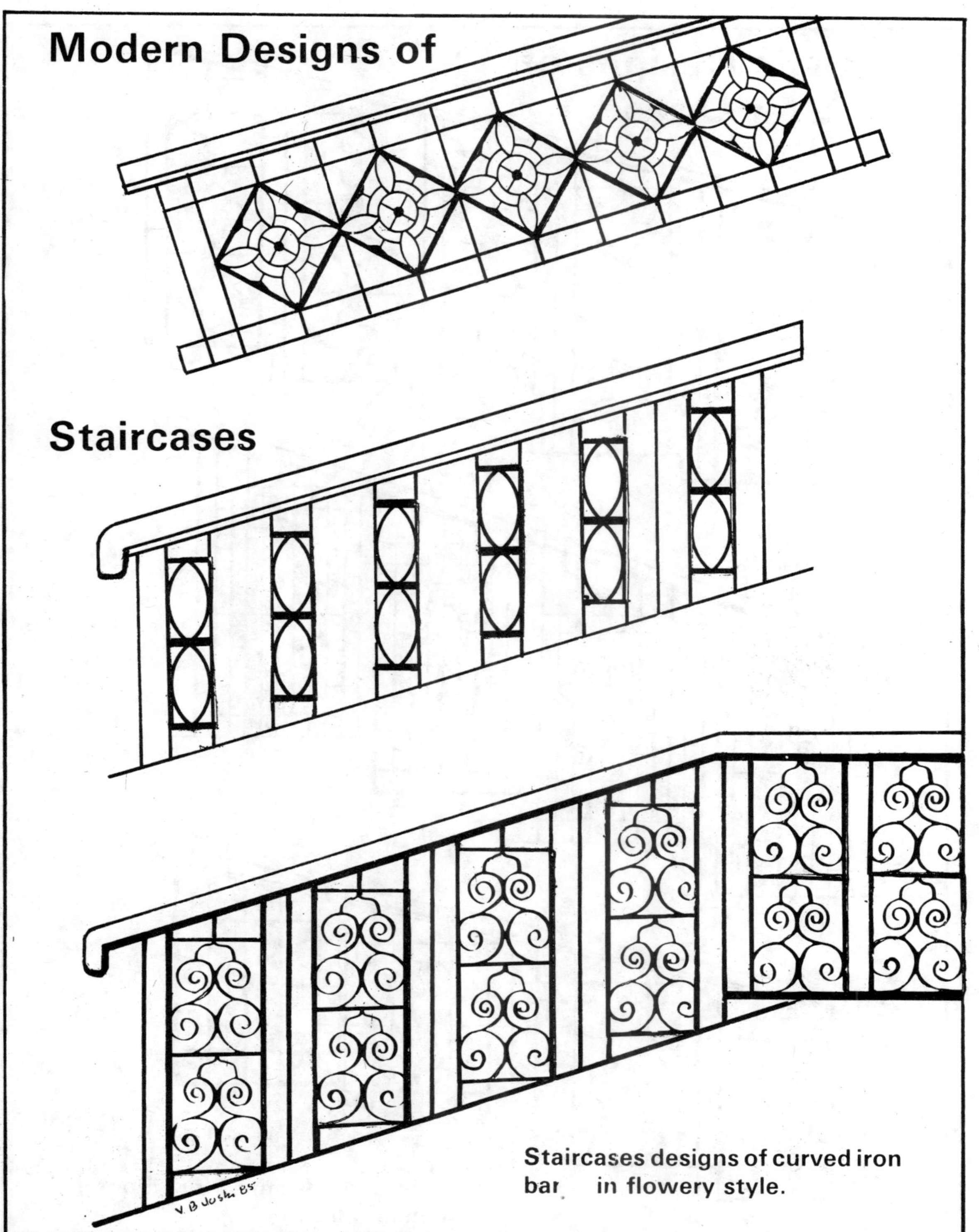

Staircases designs of curved iron bar in flowery style.

Artistic Designs of Staircases

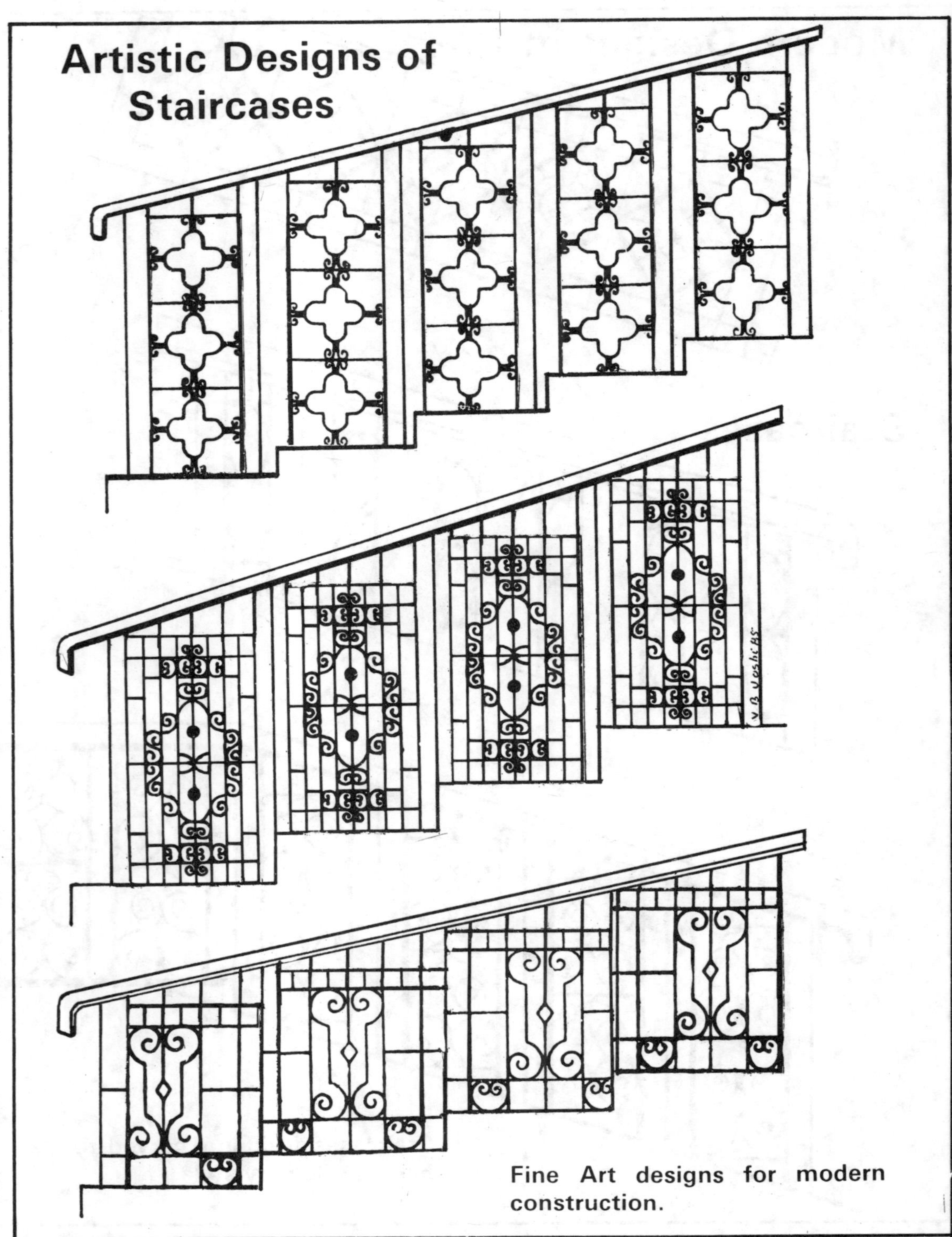

Fine Art designs for modern construction.

Artistic Designs of Staircases

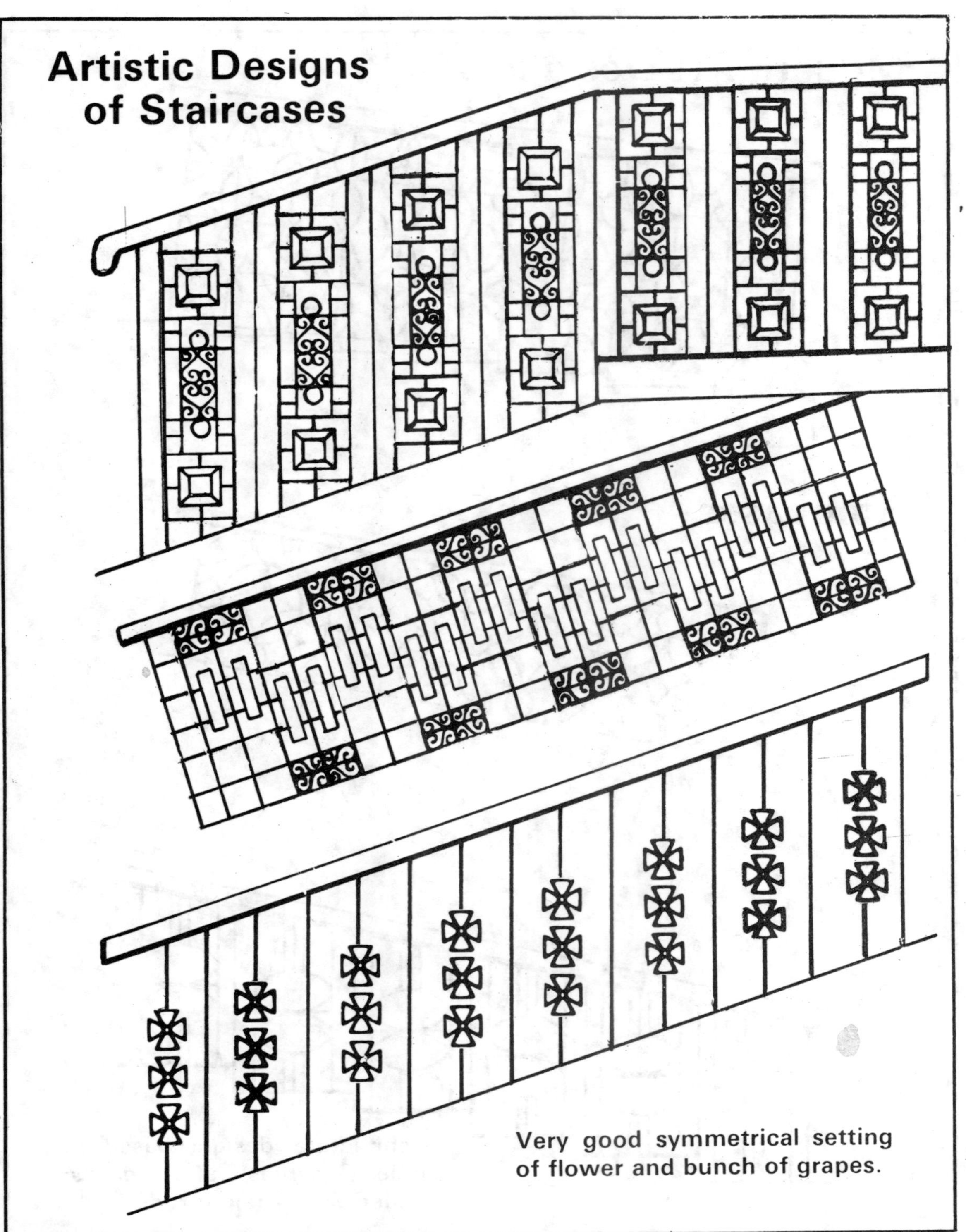

Very good symmetrical setting of flower and bunch of grapes.

Modern Art Designs of Staircases

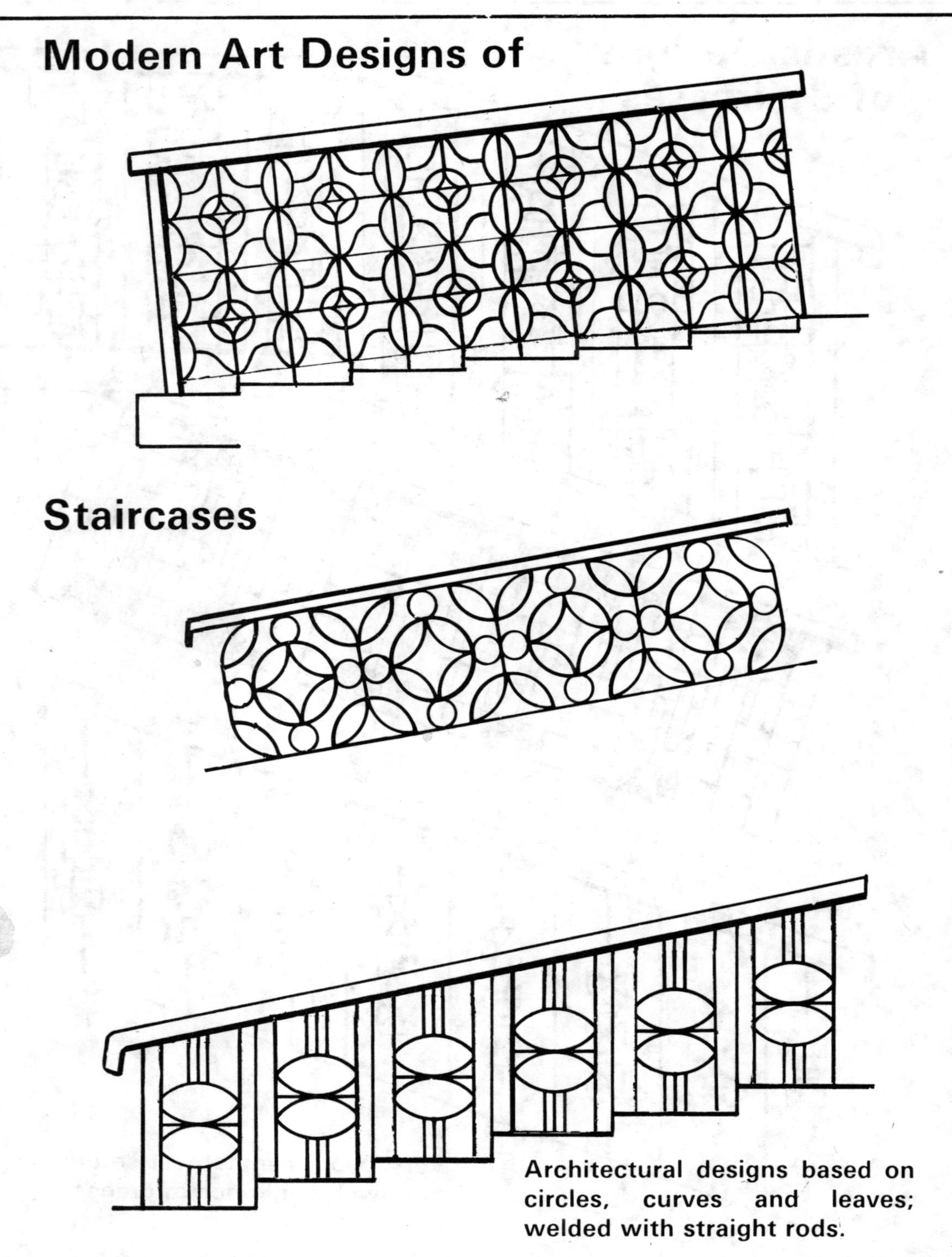

Architectural designs based on circles, curves and leaves; welded with straight rods.

Modern Art Designs of Staircases

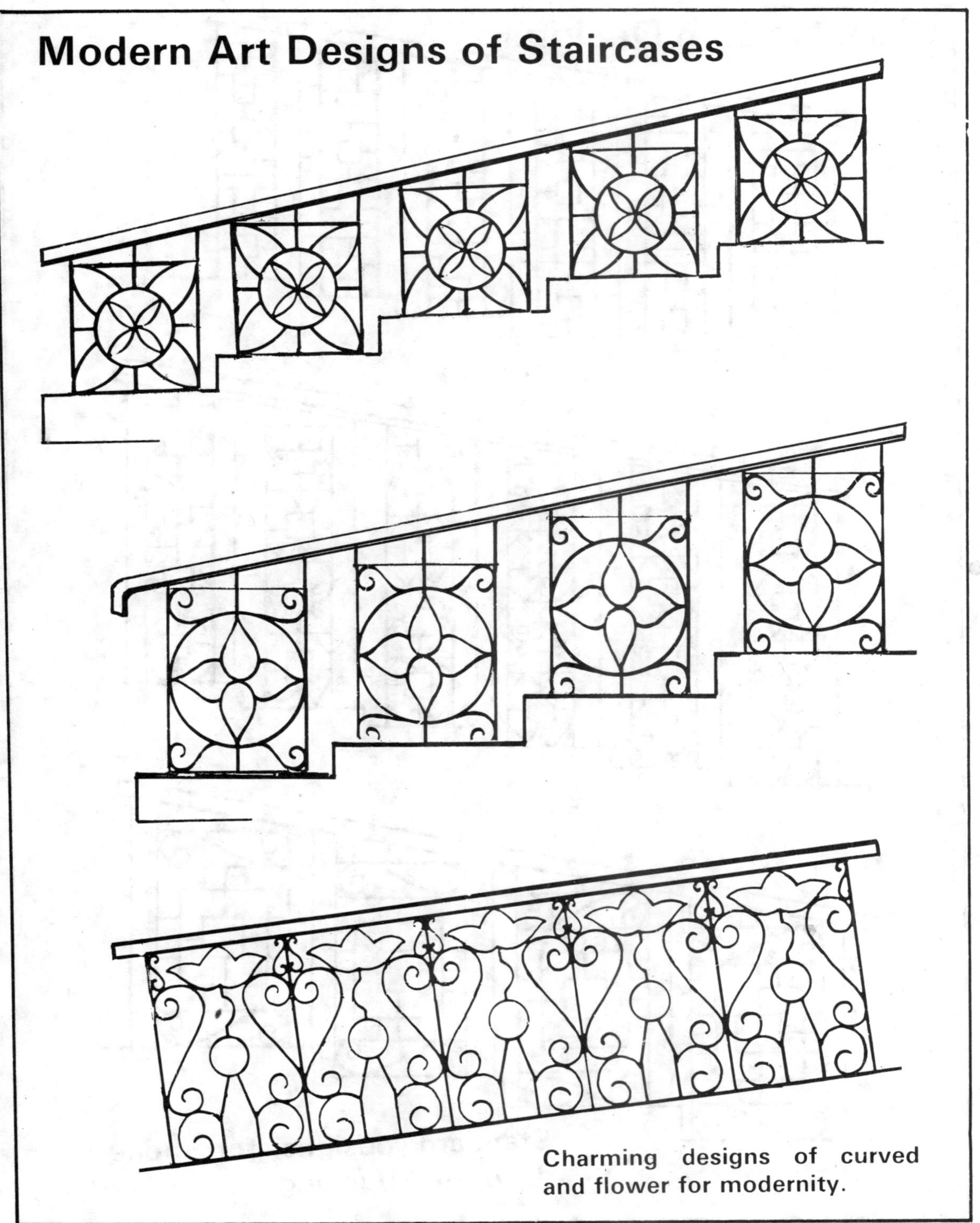

Charming designs of curved and flower for modernity.

Ultra Modern Designs

Standard designs for modern decorated building.

Artistic Designs of Staircases

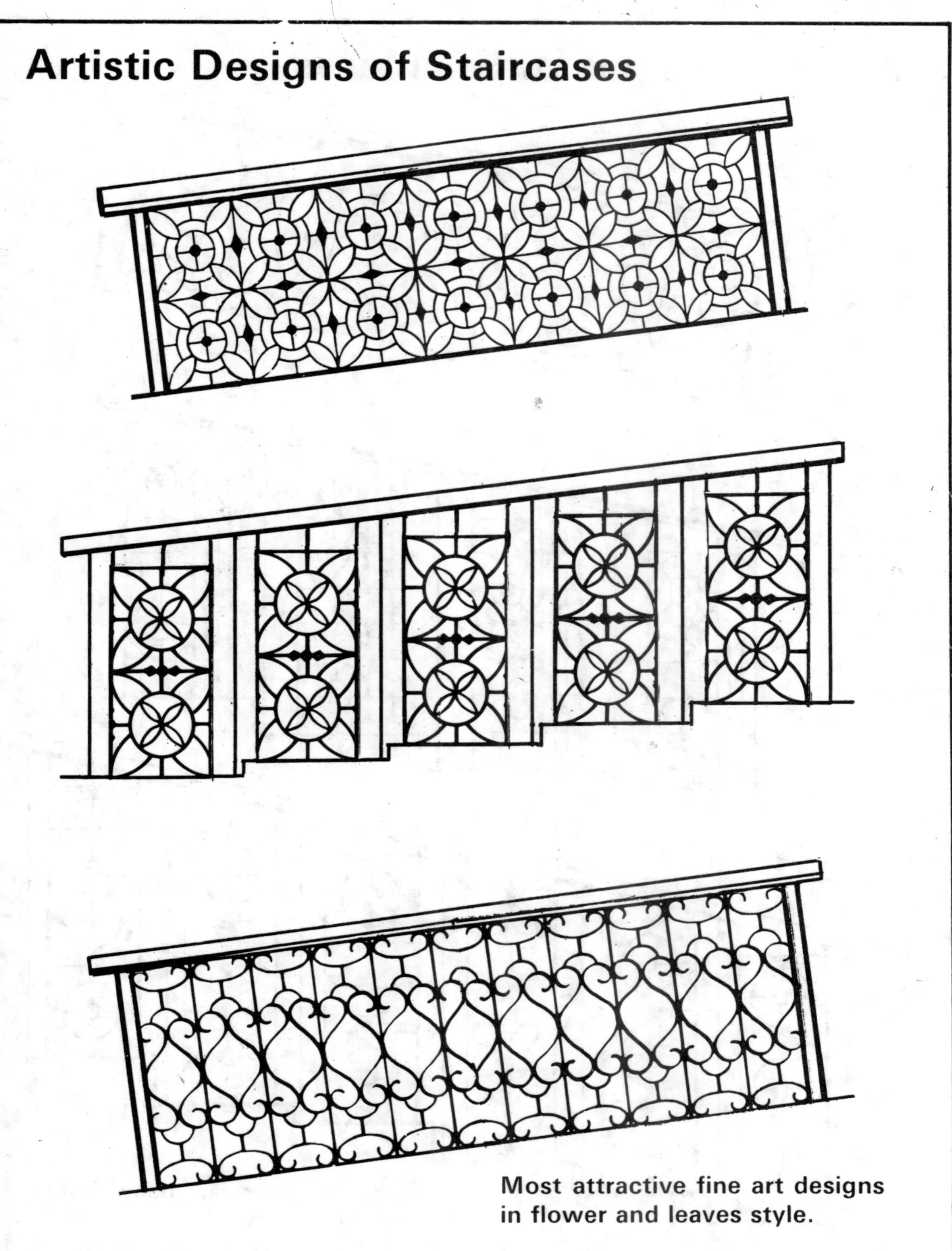

Most attractive fine art designs in flower and leaves style.

Artistic Designs of Staircases

Famous American designs for new decoration.

Modern designs of small pieces of hollow and solid pipe and rods.

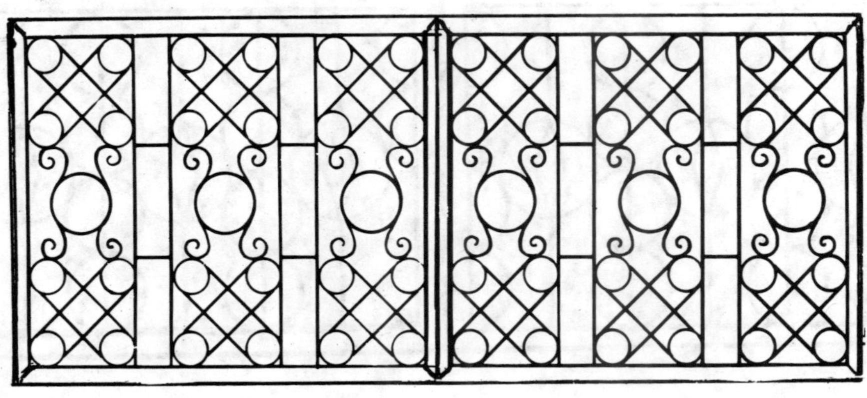

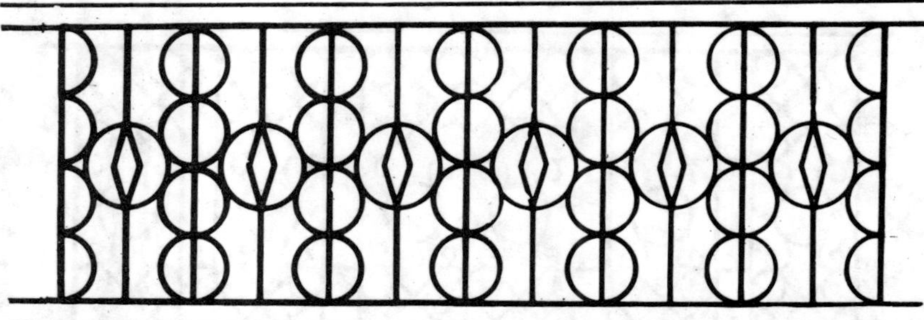

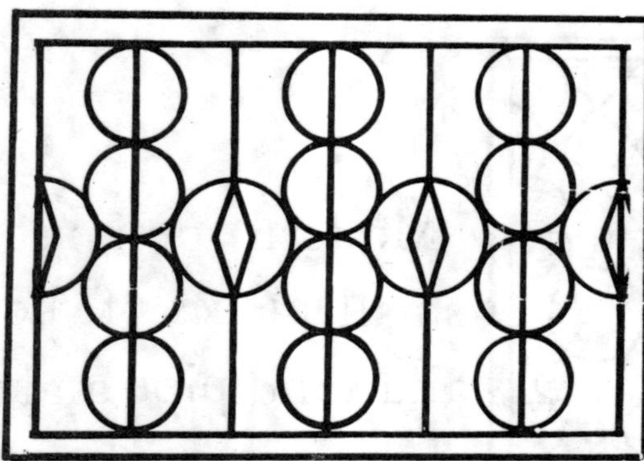

A Common design of Gates for Small and Big Factories

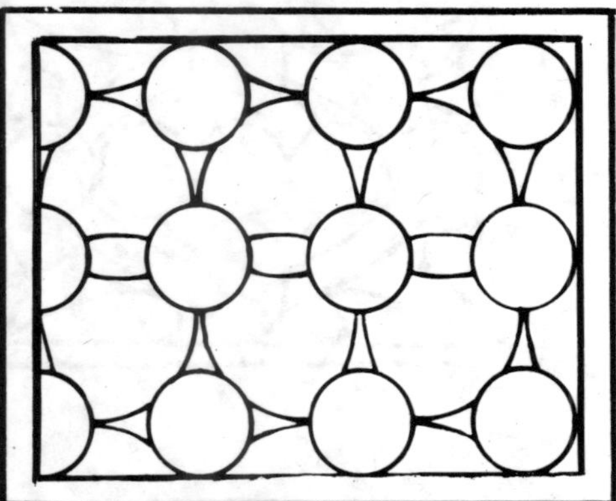
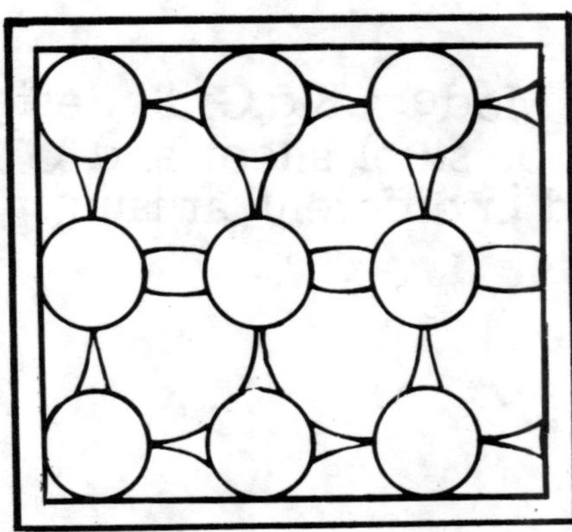

Round Iron bar designs
in layer style,
welded on the frames

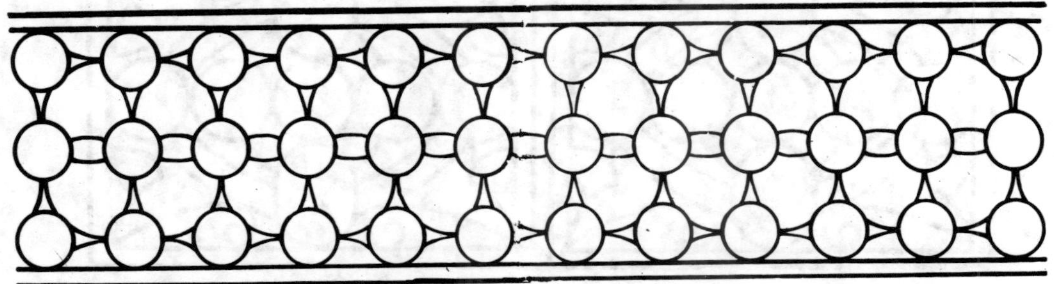

Quite Modern Big Grills design made of steel sheet and ▬ welded in different artistic style.

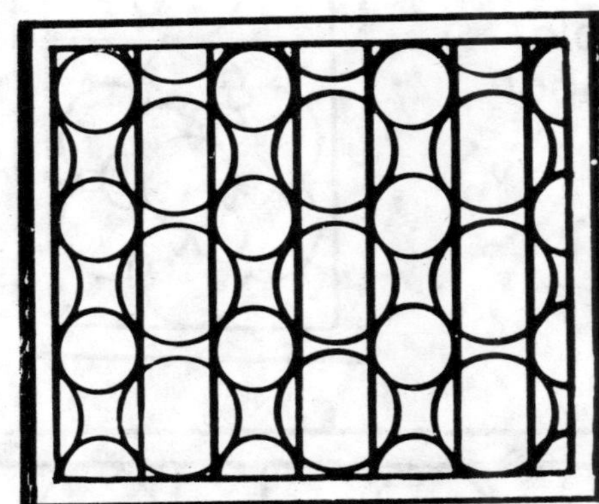

Vertical Iron bars designs for well Planned Building.

These designs shows the Idea of British Ancient Art suitable for office, College and School Buildings

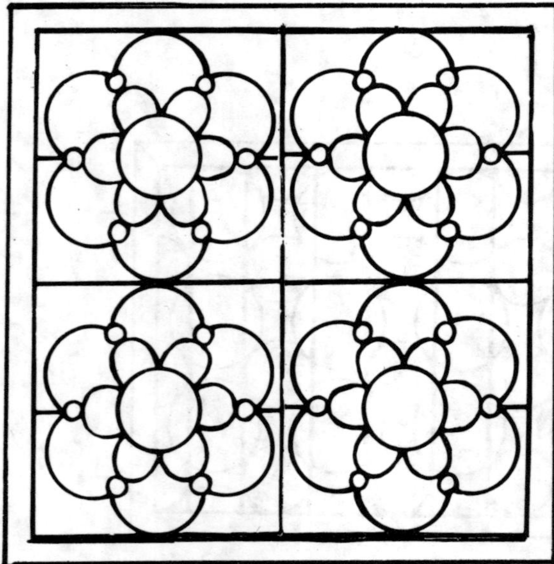

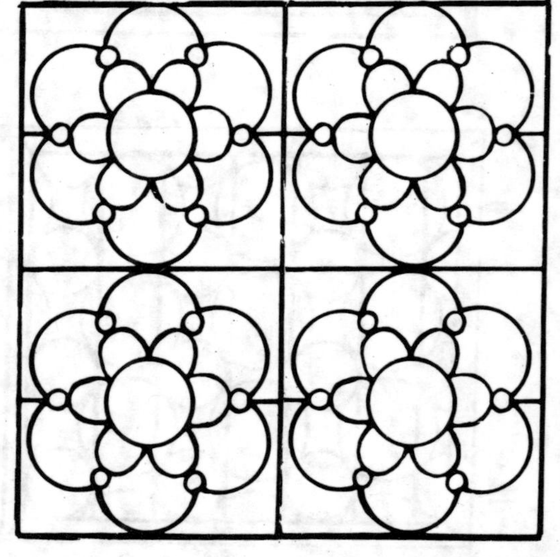

Leaves welded in-between simple circles are the main characteristi of this design.

This complete design gives idea and art of the Mughal period.

West Germany's Designs of Windows and Ventilators for New Decoration.

Australian design of Gate, Window and Railing Grills for Newly Constructed House.

New designs of bars Curved and welded in different artistic style.

Ultra-modern designs of Japan. Made of thick and thin solid rods welded in geometrical principle.

Best and latest design of modern style.

Australian design of Gate, Window and Railing Grills.

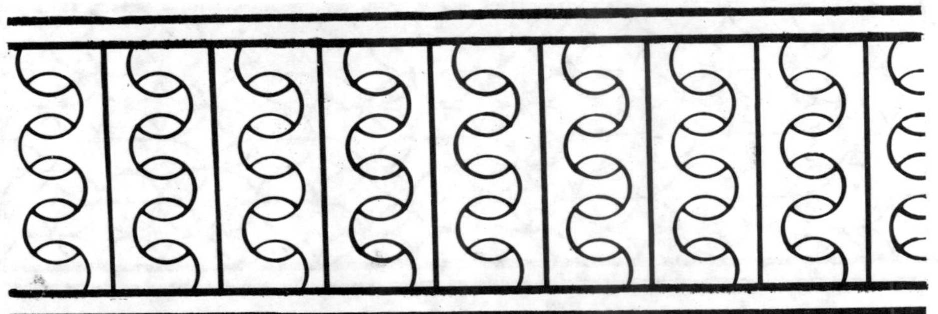

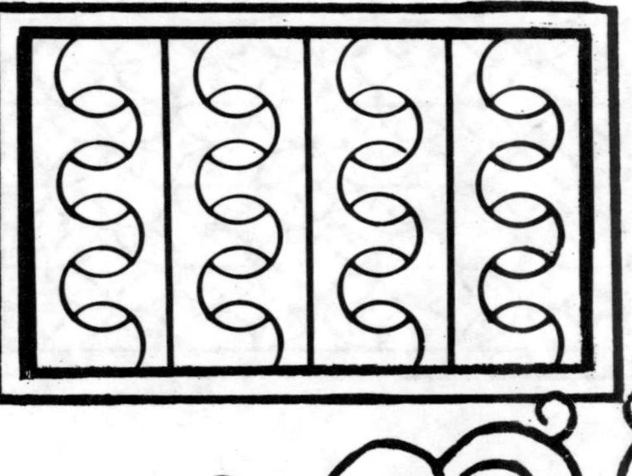

Best and latest design of modern style.

Charming design of leaves and rings for modernity.

West Germany's Designs
Windows and Ventilators

A composition of
modern design

British architectural Gate Designs of Long Iron bars welded with pipes, for Big Embassy.

Charming design of leaves and rings for modernity.

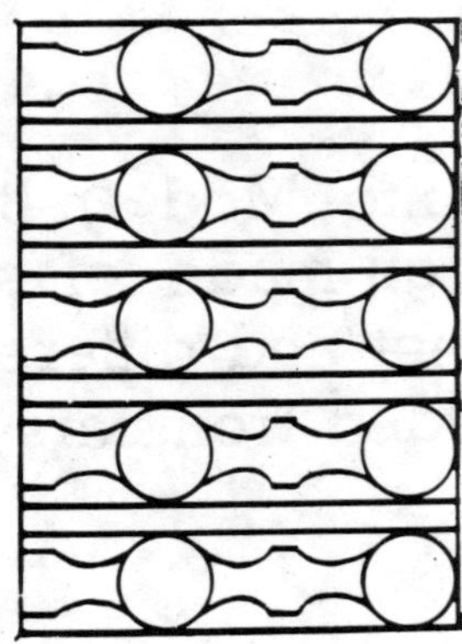

Round Iron bar designs in layer style, welded on the frames of Pipes,

Quite Modern Big design made of steel sheet and different solid Iron bars

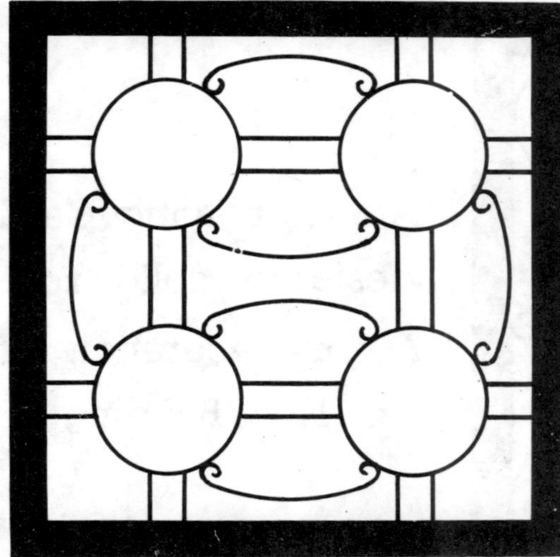

Thick and thin vertical Iron bar designs for big houses

Best playing Cards design of solid Iron bars for decoration of New Building.

Latest design of door grills of Germany's style.

Thick and thin vertical Iron bar Designs for big factories.

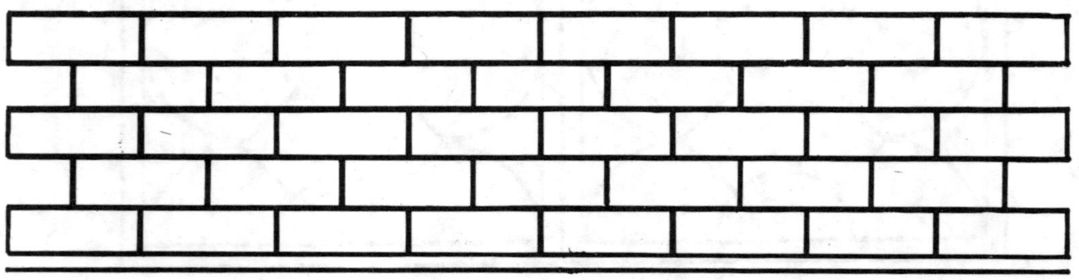

Latest design of door grills of Germany's style. welded in Geometrical principle.

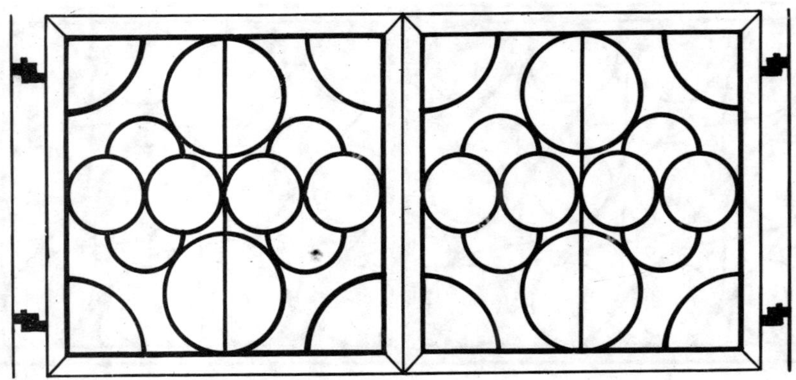

U. K. design of Gate, window and railing for new construction.

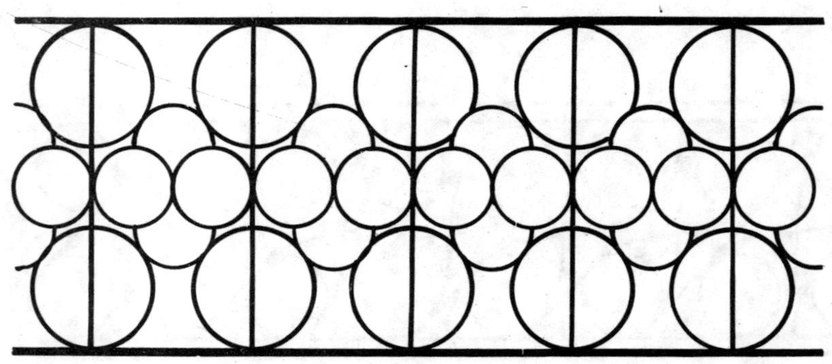

Charming design of leaves and rings for modernity.

New designs of bars, Curved and welded in different artistic style.

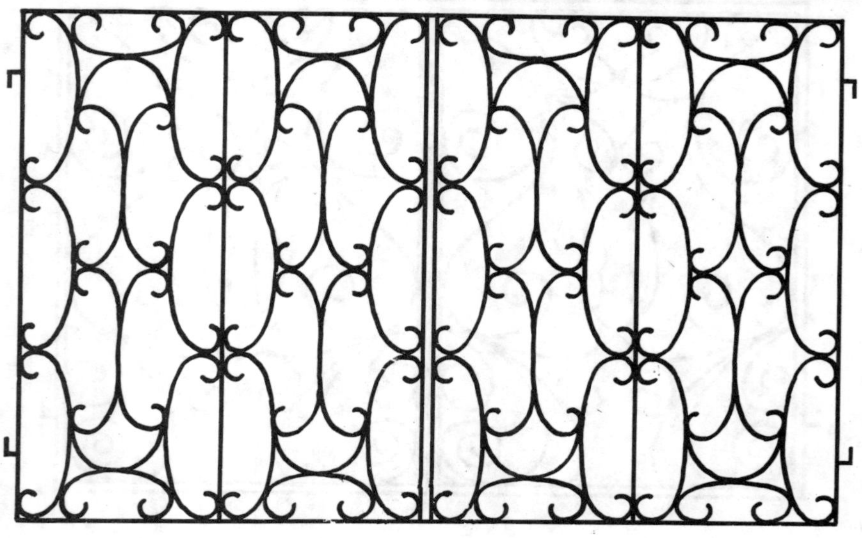

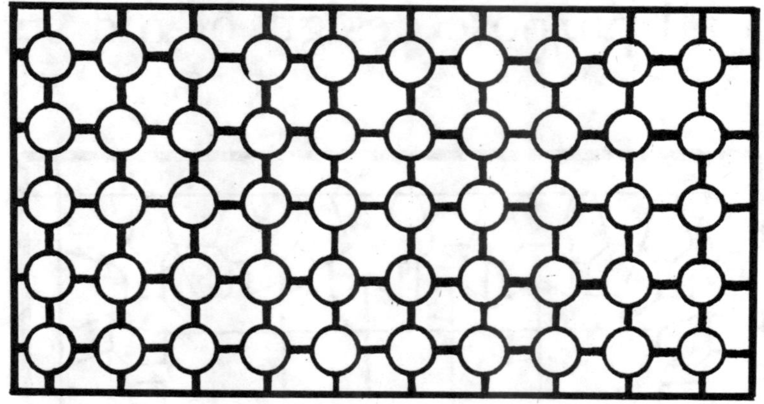

Ancient Design of Grills increases the beauty of Small or Big Building.

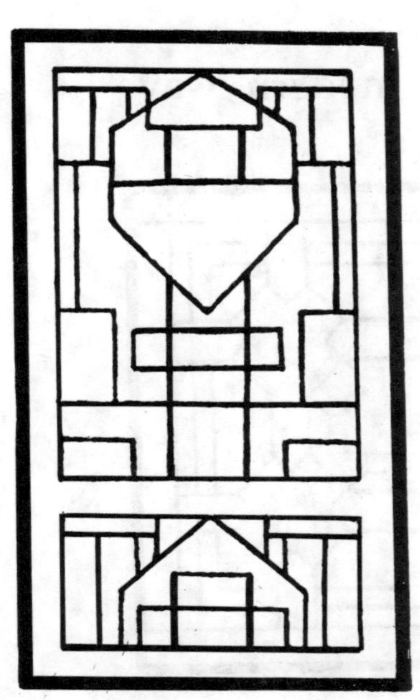

Two all purpose designs of old style.

Two leaves design fitted in modern way.

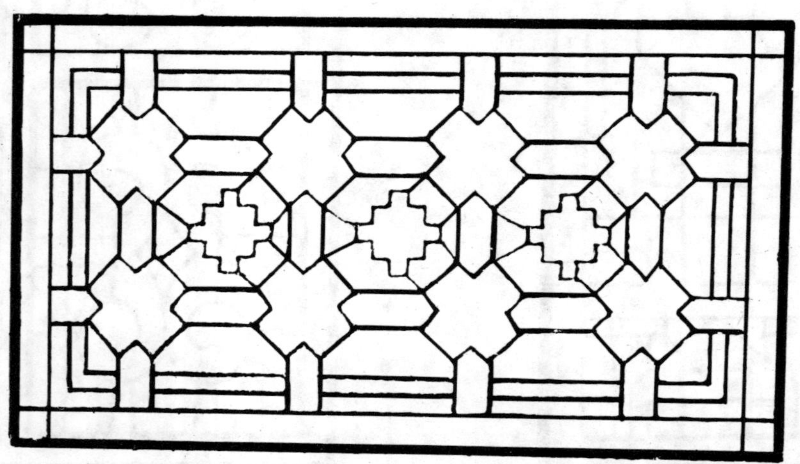

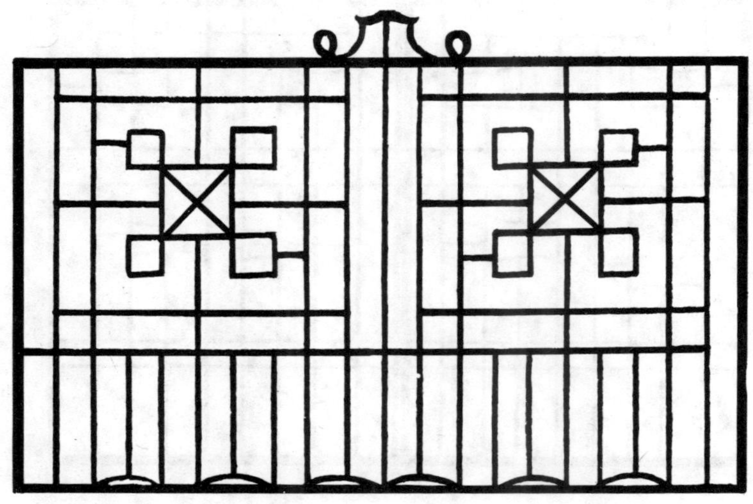

Modern Big Gate design
made of steel sheet and solid Iron bars

Round Iron bar designs in layer style, welded on the frames